# Praise for *Spiritual Rhythms in C~*

"In *Spiritual Rhythms in Communit*, ... ... ...-d journey in gentle and courageous way ... ...ut into the world in unforced rhythms of ...

**JANET O. HAGBERG,** spiritual director and ... *journey*

"Needed help for a culture out of rhythm with its soul. Sometimes we must move fast; Keith shows us how to do so from a satisfied soul."

**BILL HULL,** author of *Choose the Life*

"In *Spiritual Rhythms in Community,* Keith Meyer offers us a critical insight not found anywhere else: spiritual disciplines are not only supposed to help us become more Christlike but they are best done in community and are to send us forth on mission. Meyer puts flesh and bones on this threefold insight with the practical exercises he offers. Anyone on the spiritual journey would be wise to have this guidebook in their backpack!"

**ALBERT HAASE,** O.F.M., author of *Coming Home to Your True Self*

"Juggling the pressures of culture, technology, media, work and family is something few of us can do alone or by accident. We need intentionality and a guide. Keith Meyer's *Spiritual Rhythms in Community* offers tools for ordering the 'to-dos' of life with your hunger for God. It's practical, down to earth, personal and engaging."

**ADELE CALHOUN,** copastor, Redeemer Community Church, and author of *Invitations from God*

"Meyer makes the ancient and deeply formative ways of the early church present and possible for us today. Full of stories and examples from real life, *Spiritual Rhythms in Community* translates the often burdensome courses of ordinary existence into both the times and the means for spiritual growth and rich Christian experience."

**PHYLLIS TICKLE,** compiler of *The Divine Hours*

"Keith Meyer is a visionary practitioner. Since I first met him, in every setting in which he serves, this vision has been the abiding energy of his life and ministry. In his book, you'll learn from one who has gone there himself."

**MINDY CALIGUIRE,** author of *Discovering Soul Care*

"I consider Keith Meyer to be a wonderful friend. I also consider him to be a rare combination of megachurch pastor, spiritual pilgrim and engaging communicator. So it is no surprise that I think his latest book, *Spiritual Rhythms in Community*, is his best yet. What a wonderful job of placing the Christian disciplines in the context of community."

**GARY W. MOON**, executive director, Dallas Willard Center for Christian Spiritual Formation, and author of *Apprenticeship with Jesus*

"Spiritual rhythms are meant to bring us into fresher and deeper experiences of God, community and mission, yet in our busy world with so many distractions we often fail to make these connections. In this important book, Keith Meyer explores the rhythms of prayer and solitude that are at the core of a deeper faith. I heartily recommend it to all who are seeking greater intimacy with God."

**CHRISTINE SINE**, executive director, Mustard Seed Associates

"With the humble heart of a pastoral storyteller, Keith mentors us in the beautiful ways of quiet contemplation and social engagement."

**NATHAN FOSTER**, professor, Spring Arbor University, and author of *Wisdom Chaser*

"*Spiritual Rhythms in Community* provides profound yet tender and accessible guidance on how to live our life with God. It gives us a vivid presentation of Jesus as one who led a rich life of ordered practices and who led his immediate followers into those practices. For those who trust him, he is the door into a life of grace framed by disciplines. There his promises are fulfilled: our day-to-day life becomes a safe and abundant place to dwell. The guidance given is received from the author's experiences in such a life and from his work with many others under his instruction. That makes it realistic. The use of Scripture (especially the Psalms) that he encourages is beautiful and powerful."

**DALLAS WILLARD**, author of *Hearing God*

"Keith Meyer is on a journey with Jesus—in the local congregation, in the scholastic academy, in the self-employment business—in short, in the real world. *Spiritual Rhythms in Community* is a worthwhile and important post from his road, reminding us of the disciplines for personal formation and introducing us to relational practices that we need. It is a commendable guide for the journey inward and the journey outward, personally and in community."

**LYLE SMITH GRAYBEAL**, coordinator, Renovaré USA

# SPIRITUAL RHYTHMS IN COMMUNITY

*Being Together in the Presence of God*

# KEITH MEYER

IVP Books

An imprint of InterVarsity Press
Downers Grove, Illinois

*InterVarsity Press*
*P.O. Box 1400, Downers Grove, IL 60515-1426*
*World Wide Web: www.ivpress.com*
*E-mail: email@ivpress.com*

*InterVarsity Press® is the book-publishing division of InterVarsity Christian Fellowship/USA®, a movement of students and faculty active on campus at hundreds of universities, colleges and schools of nursing in the United States of America, and a member movement of the International Fellowship of Evangelical Students. For information about local and regional activities, write Public Relations Dept., InterVarsity Christian Fellowship/USA, 6400 Schroeder Rd., P.O. Box 7895, Madison, WI 53707-7895, or visit the IVCF website at <www.intervarsity.org>.*

*All Scripture quotations, unless otherwise indicated, are taken from the* Holy Bible, New International Version®. NIV®. *Copyright ©1973, 1978, 1984 by International Bible Society. Used by permission of Zondervan Publishing House. All rights reserved.*

*Parts of chapter eight were first published in "Go to God Like a Cigarette: Unconventional Spiritual Advice from a Surprised Pastor,"* Conversations Journal 5, *no. 1 (Spring 2007): 79-81.*

*Cover design: Cindy Kiple*
*Cover images: © Lisa Howarth/Trevillion Images*
*Interior image:* Storm on the Sea, *Brother Claude Lane, www.printeryhouse.org*

*ISBN 978-0-8308-3561-4*

*Printed in the United States of America* ∞

**Library of Congress Cataloging-in-Publication Data**

*Meyer, Keith, 1955-*
  *Spiritual rhythms in community: being together in the presence of*
*God/Keith Meyer.*
    *p. cm.*
  *Includes bibliographical references (p. )*
  *ISBN 978-0-8308-3561-4*
  *1. Contemplation. 2. Spiritual life. I. Title.*
  *BV5091.C7M494 2011*
  *248.4—dc23*

*2011047337*

| P | 19 | 18 | 17 | 16 | 15 | 14 | 13 | 12 | 11 | 10 | 9 | 8 | 7 | 6 | 5 | 4 | 3 | 2 | 1 |
| Y | 28 | 27 | 26 | 25 | 24 | 23 | 22 | 21 | 20 | 19 | 18 | 17 | 16 | 15 | 14 | 13 | 12 |

To those I have been with and led on retreat—pastors and their lay leaders, marketplace leaders and seminary students, colearners of Christ's rhythms together with their communities—may your lives be sacred space where exists an ever-expanding dance of heavenly joy arm in arm with the Father, Son and Spirit, reaching out to embrace others for life in the divine kingdom dream.

*Get away with me. . . . Walk with me and*
*work with me—watch how I do it.*
*Learn the unforced rhythms of grace.*
MATTHEW 11:28-29 (*THE MESSAGE*)

*The house of my soul is too narrow for thee to come in to me;*
*let it be enlarged by thee. It is in ruins; do thou restore it.*
AUGUSTINE

*A growing community must integrate three elements: a life of silent prayer,*
*a life of service and above all of listening to the poor, and a*
*community life through which all its members*
*can grow in their own gift.*
JEAN VANIER

# CONTENTS

# PRELUDE

*Going to a Place Where You Can Be Found*

*F*ather Harry Grant was lost and was getting anxious that he wouldn't be able to find his way back to the retreat center in time for the next session he was scheduled to lead. Having given the retreat participants their meditative work for the rest of the afternoon, he was free to do some praying of his own. So he started slowly walking the gravel paths that encircled the retreat grounds and lay just short of the surrounding forest. Meandering his way along the familiar footpaths of the retreat grounds was a favorite and familiar discipline.

It worked like a labyrinth with its twists and turns, and gave Father Harry just enough rhythm to his walk to allow him to meditate and let the path guide his feet. He was free to concentrate as he turned over the phrases of his favorite psalm, slowly repeated the Lord's Prayer or practiced what he had just been preaching, simply being and "doing nothing at all." Today that meant putting one foot in front of the other and listening to the crunching of the path's pebbles under his shoes.

Soon he was wandering off the gravel path and making his way into the woods on a beaten down path he knew very well, as he had often done before at this particular spot. His steps treated him to the sounds of crackling leaves and the snapping of fallen branches. The cooler air under this canopy of trees brought relief to his sweaty face. But he never ventured too deep into these woods, being careful to avoid where it was thick and hard to navigate. He went just far enough to be soothed by the solitude found in a cathedral of trees and the hushed stillness created by the tent of limbs and leaves. He came slowly to a halt and just stood there.

The silence began to wrap around him, broken only occasionally by the gentle shushing of the wind in the treetops, the staccato chatter of a squirrel, the drumming of a woodpecker or screech of a hawk. It transported him to another place, the cell in his heart, letting his body and mind rest and giving himself room to just be—in the cradling embrace of God's creation. This was what one of his favorite authors, Thomas Merton, called "wasting time with God," or what to those caught up in busyness might term "an unproductive downtime." But to him it had become a habit that restored his soul and made him alive to God.

After standing in this sacred space long enough to lose track of how many minutes had passed by, his reverie was interrupted. He noticed a slight dip in temperature, which brought a tiny shiver to his body, enough to wake him out of the tranquility of his reverie. He wondered if he should start heading back toward the chapel to give the next "conference," or talk, part of the Ignatian exercises, a series of meditations on Christ's life.

As he turned back, taking his time because he was reluctant to leave his holy woods, he reviewed in his mind a conference talk he had given so many times that he now almost knew it by heart. But after some time, he realized that he was taking far too long getting out of the woods. So he picked up his pace, waiting for a sign of the edge of the woods where he would re-enter the paths of the retreat grounds. With the warmth of the late afternoon sun waning and the chill of late fall in upstate Minnesota beginning to tingle his face and hands, he sensed a bit of panic. Would he be able to find his way back? And could he avoid the awkwardness of a search for him that would interrupt the retreat's rhythms? But that wasn't the real source of his irritation and slight embarrassment at being lost.

Father Harry was blind. He had been most of his life. But by his keen sense of space he had learned to get around by himself in familiar settings like this. Every time he had done this trek he had easily found his way out, always managing to find the path again. He was a little proud of how he could navigate his way into his private chapel of trees and out again. He would never hear the end of this from his coworkers, friends and family.

As he kept on walking he felt he was getting more lost and his fear of embarrassment gave way to the possibility of spending the night alone in the forest without a coat, hat or covering. He shook off that thought and the irrational fear of death by hypothermia, reassuring himself that eventually they would find him—he couldn't have gone that far. But what would he do in the meantime to keep himself from wandering farther away?

He decided he would practice "centering prayer" to clear his mind and calm him down while he waited for someone to notice he was gone. Standing still, he re-entered the cell of his heart, detaching from thoughts of being lost or of his life ending out here. This prayer of "being" was one he used regularly in prayer or in daily circumstances, like waiting in long lines. It kept his spirit available to God, helped him to be less self-obsessed and reduced his annoyance with others or impatient with life's frequent roadblocks.

It consisted of slowing down his breathing and then repeating a word like *mercy* or the name of Jesus until he had found himself once again in the cell of his quiet heart. His purpose in doing so wasn't to get anything out of it but to simply be, much as he had done a while ago in his reverie. He would wait out this unwelcome detour to his plans by simply dwelling in the safety of God's presence and start back out of the woods when he was more peaceful. But this time he did get something, a surprising thought that came to his consciousness, at first startling him and then prompting him to some action.

The thought was so strong it seemed like a voice from somewhere saying, "Just go to a place where you can be found."

It made sense but trusting it would involve some risk. If he was farther in than he thought, perhaps he could get to a road he knew was nearby and flag down a car    but he could just as easily get more lost. Should he trust the nudging of this voice? Like many times in his life, what appeared as divine help had to be met with faith; he did not have the certainty of a command to obey, only a gentle invitation to follow into the insecurity of trusting.

He took the invitation and began to step out to follow. The road that he knew was somewhere nearby would most likely be in more open space, which he could sense by tapping the trees with his cane and by the remaining warmth of the afternoon sun's rays. With his senses of hearing and feeling now fully engaged, he slowly moved on and eventually reached the graveled shoulder of a road. After standing there for a while, he heard the sound of tires becoming louder. Waving his arms to flag the driver, he was cheerfully given a ride back to the retreat center.

Father Harry never forgot the lesson of being lost in the woods and the direction to "just go to a place where you can be found." It became a metaphor for his favorite talk on why we practice spiritual disciplines, for they are places where we can go to recover our life and be found by God and others.

# INTRODUCTION

## *The Trinitarian Two-Step*

*M*y wife is a junior high school health and physical education teacher who loves to teach her students how to dance all kinds of dances, from fast-paced square dances to slower waltzes. I have two left feet and find dancing awkward, but I humor my wife when we are at a restaurant with a band and dance floor by going out for the obligatory one or two slow dances. When Cheri and I were facing the empty nest, we decided we needed to learn something the other liked to do to fill some of the time we had enjoyed with our kids' activities. I picked golf for Cheri, and you guessed it, she picked dancing for me.

She needed to brush up on her square dancing, and so we joined a square dance club for a couple of months. Contrary to my expectations, I came to enjoy it. I found dancing to be easier than I expected. When I got the rhythms of engaging my partner by stepping toward her, taking her hand or putting an arm around her waist and then letting go, and then coordinating this with a whole group of people, it was surprisingly fun. I found that dancing is a series of engaging and disengaging rhythms that can be learned. And the same is true for the disciplines of developing rhythms for a life full of God's power, love and joy with others—the life of the Trinity.

## THE DANCE OF THE TRINITY

I often tell the Father Harry story that appears in the preface to illustrate how the disciplines work in our lives as rhythms of *disengagement* and *engagement*. We can so easily get lost in the constant demands of life that we develop habits of nonstop busyness and wonder why we feel empty and isolated. We need to develop a dance of life in which we regularly *disengage* from life as usual and get away with God for rest and renewal. Then we can *engage* once again in the life and love of God and others. Life in these rhythms becomes a dance with the Trinity—Father, Son and Holy Spirit—along with all of the people around us.

John's Gospel begins its account of Jesus' ministry at a wedding party. His mother asked Jesus to help keep the party going by doing something about the dwindling supply of wine. At first he was reluctant, but I think as he prayed about it, his heavenly Father may have said, "Do what she says. A party celebrating the uniting of two individuals is the perfect way for us to show up!" So John records the Spirit's first sign of Jesus' divine mission. And from the richness of the Trinity's life, Jesus made enough wine that night to fuel not only that evening's but many evenings of wedding dances.

The Trinity's interior life is described in Greek as *perichoresis*. The word literally means to "dance around," which signifies how the three distinct persons of the Trinity relate to each other. This word, first used by the church fathers in their attempts to unfold the biblical teaching on the Trinity, describes the loving embrace, interplay and mutual work of the Father, Son and Spirit in their divine work and life together, a dance resulting in creation, redemption and someday, the consummation and restoration of all things.

Soon after that dance created the universe, we humans fell out of step. But in Jesus we are invited to join in it once again, and when we join we are to invite the whole world to dance with us. Our English word *choreography*, a plan of coordinated dance moves, has this Greek word as its root. In the chapters that follow I will suggest that we learn to take spiritual disciplines as our means or steps in *a Trinitarian two-step dance of disengagement and engagement* in order for us to live as God meant us to live.

One of my greatest surprises as I began to learn these rhythms is that Jesus is our best example of how to use the disciplines to be found by God and each other. He needed soul care just as we do. In the humility of his incarnation he had to submit to the same processes of spiritual growth and maturation that we do, and his soul-care rhythms involved the discipline of disengaging from life and ministry to be with the Father, where he was formed by the Spirit in the Father's love. Jesus' interactive life with the Father, evidenced by the short conversational prayers and his frequent references to his Father's authority, power and voice as he ministered, was the fruit of disengaging from life as usual in order to be alone and enriched by the Spirit and the Father.

And Jesus taught his disciples these same rhythms. But he didn't do it directly at first. He waited while they observed the power of his life and the rhythm of disciplines that shaped it, and then one day they said, "Teach us how to pray." They watched his dance of life with the Father and the Spirit, and they wanted to learn those dance steps.

## FOLLOWING JESUS INTO LIFE

Yes, Jesus teaches on the disciplines, but not as much as he demonstrates them in his practice. They are background in his life, not foreground. And as we follow him, we notice how he is often led by the Spirit to be alone with the Father, and then he reenters life with others full of the Spirit and the Father's presence and power. We too can ask him to teach us how to pray, to practice his life rhythms and join the dance of the Trinity. And as we do, those following us will ask to be led into the disciplines that will get them into the dance.

As you read and use the ideas in this book, it is important to note three ways it is different from other books on the disciplines.

*1. Disciplines are for dancing in life.* First, we learn from Jesus that when practicing disciplines we enter into space with God and others in order to experience life change. Too often spiritual disciplines are presented without connection with the life they are to produce. If we practice the disciplines and they don't work to make us more like the Jesus, they may have become legalistic measures misused to resist and avoid actual life change, or they can be done as performances that give us a false sense of transformation.

In the exercises of this book we will disengage from noise and talking, not just to learn how to be in quiet but to develop a quiet mind and life more open to God and others. We will disengage for a period of time from cell phones and being online not just to break the grip of these tools on our lives but to have power to use them to love others. We will engage with the poor and marginalized, not making them our service project to feel better about ourselves but to discover our common belovedness in Christ and our need for each other.

*2. Disciplines are for dancing together.* We learn from Jesus' example that spiritual disciplines are *best done in community*, where they are experienced and reflected on together—even those disciplines where we need to be alone. Far too often the spiritual disciplines are presented as private activities. Seldom are the disciplines, even those of solitude and silence, presented in the context of a shared experience with others. And yet in the context of a supportive community the more rigorous and challenging disciplines, like solitude and silence, become easier. This book is not meant to be an isolated reading experience but is designed to be a group field guide to shared practices for change in communal living.

I have found in my own life and the life of the communities I serve that practices of silence and solitude are rarely kept up and do not have a chance for long-term effect without being shared with others, at the minimum with a soul friend or spiritual director. These effects are even greater when a couple, a family, a group of friends, a church small group or team members of a staff experience being alone with God, but share that experience with each other. In the push and shove of our everyday routines, this is critical.

Jesus, our example in this book, practices solitude in community with his disciples. In Gethsemane he takes his disciples with him to the garden, to pray alone but also with his friends. In the garden he withdrew a stone's throw from the disciples but checked on them hoping that they were sharing in a mutually supportive time of being in solitude. We can follow his example by practicing disciplines together, with our families, friends and in our churches. In this way we will find and create a new kind of life together.

3. *Disciplines make dancing contagious.* We learn from Jesus that the disciplines are to work as a baseline for a life rhythm of formation for a community. This results in a powerful *mission* that sweeps others into the dance of trinitarian life. I often read books that deal only with being missional or being in community, or are only about spiritual formation and the disciplines. The problem is that these don't demonstrate an understanding of how disciplines of formation, community and mission work together. In fact, it appears that for many the three may be mutually exclusive.

This is in stark contrast to Jesus, who, as we watch him in the incarnated dance of his life and ministry with the Father, Spirit and others, is our teacher and example of how to enter and live in these rhythms. His rich prayer life and the formation of a missional community of twelve (and more) are our model. I find that students who do the exercise in the first chapter of this book are startled at the amount of time Jesus spends in prayer and how it links him to his community and fuels his mission.

Most of us know that Jesus spent time alone in prayer, but we are unaware that in his hectic last week he didn't decrease his times of prayer, he increased them as the demands of mission increased. He not only spent one night in the garden of Gethsemane but was there all night, every night, of the last week of his life. After each night of *formation* in prayer, he went to be in *community* with his disciples and on *mission* in the temple to the crowds. And this represents a distilled concentration of a rhythm of life he had cultivated throughout his life.

These were his rhythms early on. His youthful formation in these rhythms is first evidenced with his forty days in prayer before his three years of building a community for mission to the world. Before choosing his first disciples, he spends an entire night in prayer, most likely taken up with what he does the next morning, calling to himself twelve apprentices to be his community. And they accompany him on his mission to the lost house of Israel.

The disciples are schooled for three years in that rhythm, and it becomes their own after he leaves. They do as he says and stay together praying in the upper room, being formed in prayer and empowered and reconstituted as a community by the Spirit's fire. Pouring out of that house in mission, they spoke in the tongues of the Diaspora Jews and God-fearers gathered from all over the world in Jerusalem.

The pattern is repeated as we watch the rhythms of Peter, who at the sixth hour is praying at his usual place, his rooftop. Peter prays for three hours and is deeply transformed by a vision and given a new vision and experience of community. He is sent on a mission to a Gentile who also is in prayer, being formed to join Peter in community.

Paul spends time in worship, fasting and prayer with some leaders in Antioch. In doing so he is called to the same pattern, forming a missional community to reach the Gentiles.

What began as the dance of the community of the Father, Son and Spirit, continued with the Father sending the Son by the power of the Spirit on a mission to redeem us as his beloved, and it has continued now for two thousand years, sweeping up you and me. Now we too can practice those same rhythms and catch up those around us. Whenever we practice the disciplines, it is to be better dancers in kingdom life, to keep in step with the Trinity and open our hands and hearts to those who have not yet joined the celebration.

## PSALM REFLECTIONS

Each chapter begins with a psalm reflection related to Jesus' example. There are exercises for meditation, prayer and experiencing the truth of that psalm. Psalms are the living room of the Bible, where the whole drama of God's saving work and all of human experience is displayed. If for some reason I was forced to leave behind my Bible and could take just one of its sixty-six books, I would take Psalms, for in this book I find the rest of the Bible.

The psalms deeply influenced Jesus' life and so were part of his teaching for the disciples. They were the songbook for his experiences in the temple and at the Last Supper. The psalms were on Jesus' mind in his darkest hour on the cross. They are also the most quoted portion of the Hebrew Scriptures by the New Testament writers. The psalms are a place where God's people are found in times when they are lost or distracted in life.

The psalms exercises are best done by reading the psalm a few times, not just once, before answering the questions. I suggest you read the psalm once a day for a few days. Then read the questions without answering them, letting them and the psalm saturate your being for a couple of days. Ask the Father in Jesus' name for wisdom, and ask the Holy Spirit for enlightening. Don't be afraid to call a group member with a question or to share an "aha" experience from your meditation. There will be time for sharing in the group, but when you marinate yourself in God's Word and share with another person what you are finding, God will bring you to much more than just a Bible study; he will make his Word abide in you. In Colossians 3:16 Paul says that the Word of Christ can *richly* dwell in us as a group when we take time to really meditate together.

## FINDING OUR RHYTHM

While the psalm at the beginning of each chapter provides an immediate place to practice Jesus' rhythms, the extended exercises at the end of each chapter offer more intensive experiences in living out the chapter's theme. Most of the exercises can be done in the space of a few hours, some are to be done throughout the day and week, but note that there are three exercises that will take most of a day, from morning to late afternoon, to complete. They require going on a day's field trip or retreat. Take time to review all of the exercises ahead of time so you can plan as a group and as individuals for scheduling time to complete them.

These are designed to be group experiences. They can be used with groups in formal church programming, such as small groups, staff teams or adult education classes. They also can be used by the adults and teenagers in a family, a group of friends, or a married couple. I suggest you designate a leader and coleader of your group to help the group members remember to schedule these group exercises well before you share your experience of the exercise.

As part of the book's three one-day exercises, you and those in your group will take a whole day to read the book of Luke in one sitting and then meditate on Jesus' disengagement and engagement rhythms (chapter one's day-long exercise). All of you can practice extended disengagement from electronic gadgets by going a whole day unplugged—without being online or on your cell phone—to be more in the moment, or use a day to experience the restorative sounds of silence, God's most used and first language. Together you can practice engagement by spending a day in the inner city with those on the margins. Or you can let a child take you on a nature walk or engage in play and be more present in the moment. Or you can learn to journal on each other's hearts and take a prayer flight together over the whole world, praying for everyone on earth.

(See the appendix for group leaders for more ideas about reading this book with others.)

# *Part One*

# THE RHYTHMS
## OF DISENGAGEMENT

*I*n part one we will first *disengage* from all that keeps us from a life with God and others in order to hear God's call to become apprentices. In part two, we will *engage* in our unique call to go and make apprentices of Jesus. The first step in the dance of disengagement disciplines begins by joining Jesus in his custom of regularly taking long periods of time to be with his Father to hear his voice proclaim his pleasure in us as God's beloved children. These times and places of practicing the presence of the Father will eventually create a retreat center of sacred space and time in our bodies. And this retreat center of the heart will be deepened as we go into the desert of our postmodern world with the ancient fathers and mothers.

We can become strong enough to be free of our addiction to the electronic virtual world and enter into the real presence of God and others. Learning to live increasingly in the moment, we can break out of the prison of our productivity and begin to see the value in doing nothing for an afternoon or whole day and find that in doing so we restore our souls and rediscover the greater meaning of our lives— who we are, not just what we do. Finally, we will learn to stop using words and to be quiet to begin to hear God's first language, silence. In that silence we become quiet enough to listen to God and others, the calm of our lives being a refuge from life's storms. And when we lose that quiet, we know where to go to be found again.

## The Father's Good Shepherding: Psalm 23

The LORD is my shepherd, I shall not be in want.
 He makes me lie down in green pastures,
he leads me beside quiet waters,
 he restores my soul.
He guides me in paths of righteousness
 for his name's sake.
Even though I walk
 through the valley of the shadow of death,
I will fear no evil,
 for you are with me;
your rod and your staff,
 they comfort me.

You prepare a table before me
 in the presence of my enemies.
You anoint my head with oil;
 my cup overflows.
Surely goodness and love will follow me
 all the days of my life,
and I will dwell in the house of the LORD
 forever.

THIS IS ONE OF THE FIRST PASSAGES of Scripture I memorized as a child. I still wake up at night and find myself praying it in response to something that is threatening to disturb my peace in God. It reminds me that the universe is God's pasture and that there is no situation or place in life where I am alone. I can count on his provision, restoration and goodness because I am his.

Jesus is never recorded as directly quoting this psalm, but its images of shepherd and sheep, dinner host and guests fill his teaching and parables in Luke's Gospel about the character of God. Jesus described the Father's shepherd care for us when he said, "Do not be afraid, little flock, for your Father has been pleased to give you the kingdom" (Luke 12:32). I believe that the truths of Psalm 23 (as well as other teachings of the Hebrew Scriptures on the Father's shepherding) composed a large part of Jesus' formation, as he experienced God's care for him and then modeled that care for his own disciples.

In Psalm 23 there are two images, God as our Shepherd (vv. 1-4) through life, and God as our Host for a banquet of life (vv. 5-6). Good shepherds and hosts *know* the conditions and needs of their sheep or guests. They *cherish* or value their flocks and shower their attention and best efforts on them. They do whatever they can to *bless* or enhance those under their care so that they flourish.

- What needs of the sheep/guests does the Shepherd/Host *know* must be met? How does the Shepherd/Host show that he deeply loves and *cherishes* those under his care? What does the Shepherd/Host's *blessing* or desire for the sheep and guests well-being look like?

- When you think of God as your Father, your Shepherd in life, what connects with you? What disconnects are there due to your earthly fathering? How well did your parents *know* you? Explain. In what ways did they *cherish* you? How did they *bless* you and your gifts and dreams for life? Who else did God use to know, cherish and bless you?

- In what ways do you long to be known, cherished and blessed by God the Father? Pray that God will answer these longings.

# Getting Alone to
# Be with the Father

*I* had never seen my father so open with his feelings. He was about to conduct the funeral service for my grandfather after leading the family in a casketside prayer service. Grandpa had been a gentle and guileless Christian soul, but didn't know, as his own father didn't know, how to be intimate with his sons. As everyone was about to leave, I asked my father if he and I could stay so I could pray for him, giving him a chance to stop being so strong and leading all of us, and for a moment to be present to his own grief. To my surprise, after my prayer, he flung himself on the casket and began to sob. After several minutes his sobbing died down. With my hands on his shoulder, he lifted himself and said in deep remorse, "I loved you, Dad. I loved you, I really loved you, and I know you loved me too. I just wish we could have said that to each other when you were here."

Father wounds are some of the most pervasive and deep wounds we can have. And for many of us these wounds are some of the deepest in our lives, taking us out of the dance of trinitarian life with others due to the critical role fathers have in teaching us the intimacy of being deeply known and understood, the self-worth due to being cherished and loved, and the blessing of our gifts and unique contribution to others. And the irony is that for many of us our dads did the best they could; they tried to communicate that love, but in our broken world they either don't say it or we can't hear it enough. Like my dad, we resolve to do better, but still fail and even repeat our own version of the same sad patterns that we have learned all our lives.

So my dad made a point to be at all my childhood sporting events. He wanted a relationship with me that he didn't have with his dad. He taught my brother and I how to throw and catch a baseball, football and basketball. He taught us how to serve and volley a ping pong ball so hard it would give our opponent a good sting if he or she missed it. He knew football and used it to be in his kids' lives. He came to as many of our summer league and after-school games as he could and was so involved with what was going on that my coach began to rely on him for his plays.

He also liked movies, despite the fact that we were in a church culture that taught that movies were sinful. He would take us to another town to go see movies like *Mary Poppins*. When I was in junior high, he took me to a movie I will never forget: *I Never Sang for My Father*. He explained that this movie illustrated his unfulfilled desire for intimacy with his own father. As the title suggests, the film is about the fierce love they bear for each other, and their inability to communicate that love, or very much of anything else. After the movie Dad explained what in the movie had touched in him, how he too had longed for his father's love and participation in his life, and the desire he had that we boys could have something different with him, intimacy and deep relationship. His dad never came to any of his activities. And so my dad made it a point to be with us in ours.

The film opens with the son pondering the death of his parent with a soliloquy, saying, "Death ends a life, but it does not end a relationship, which struggles on in the survivor's mind toward some resolution which it may never find." This is so true. And in our family there have been generations of unresolved father-to-child relationships. My image of God as my Father is filtered through that family history. And I did hear my father's "I love you." He made sure that he did that. But the relationship between us was still inadequate. We still work on it to this day.

Our relationships (or the lack of them) with our parents—their quality and the unresolved issues—are often the primary and foundational stuff of our interior-life work. If we don't know we are loved by Mom and Dad, we don't know if anyone can love us. My dad moved the ball forward on the field of our family's father-son heritage, and I am trying with my children to do the same. But later in life, he admitted to being distracted through workaholism and ministry burnout, which caught him up in the very family dysfunction he wanted to avoid.

Yes, father wounds are some of the most damaging for children and their own families. But they point to a deeper need, one that no earthly father could ever meet, our need to know the love of our heavenly Father.

## JESUS, THE SON WHO BRINGS US INTO FATHERLY BELOVEDNESS

It is interesting and profound that the last verse of the Old Testament, Malachi 4:6, is about the relationship of fathers to their children. This promise of the gospel's power to heal and deliver the broken and alienated family ends the Hebrew Scriptures and gives us a peek into what Jesus would bring. God promised to turn "the hearts of the fathers to their children, and the hearts of the children to their fathers" (Malachi 4:6 NASB). Paul and the writer of Hebrews makes it clear that human fathering is second best to heavenly fathering. In Ephesians 3, Paul prays to the Father from whom all fatherhood on earth has its origin, and Hebrews makes it clear that our earthly father's care for us at best is just a taste of what our heavenly Father's eternal care is all about. Luke even reminds us that if our earthly fathers give us good things when we ask, we should expect even better from God.

Jesus came to bring the Father's love to us to make sure we knew it, tasted it, lived from it and shared it with our own children and all God's children.

So what was Jesus' relationship with his earthly father? And how did that relationship figure into Jesus' relationship to his Father in heaven? By the time of Jesus' ministry, when he was about thirty, he had lost his father, Joseph, who is last seen when Jesus was twelve. As a preteen, he was already evidencing a strong relationship with his heavenly Father, explaining that he stayed behind in the temple because he needed to be in his "Father's house" (Luke 2:41-50).

Jesus had developed a strong sense of his heavenly Father's presence in the temple, whether on pilgrimage as a child or teenager, as a rabbi teaching on its porches about the Father, or guarding it as a place open to all for prayer to the Father. He knew the Father's presence in the temple of creation, where one fallen sparrow mattered and the wildflowers are smartly arrayed. But most of all, Jesus sensed the Father's desire to live in us and experienced his presence so powerfully that he wasn't afraid of his own body's (or temple's) destruction.

When the disciples asked Jesus to teach them to pray after one of his times of being alone with God, he directed them to address God as "Father" (Luke 11:2). Over the weeks and months they had known him, they watched his rhythm of being alone with the Father. And they had seen the fruit of his times with the Father. I believe that in those times he was alone, he was being formed by the Father as he communed with him in the Spirit, and we too can be formed in that love by learning to dance with Jesus and the Spirit as they move in step with the Father and each other.

The book of Hebrews puts it this way:

> During the days of Jesus' life on earth, he offered up prayers and petitions . . . to the one who could save him from death, and he was heard because of his reverent submission. Son though he was, he learned obedience from what he suffered and, once made perfect, he became the source of eternal salvation for all who obey him. (Hebrews 5:7-9 TNIV)

Jesus was the Son of God, but he emptied himself in some mysterious way to submit to our need for formation in God's love, so that he not only showed us God's love on the cross but also how to enter into that formation in his own soul-care rhythms.

What did Jesus hear from God in these times of prayer? What words of life fed his soul's cry for life from God, a life that would trust God to raise him from death? There are two times that we hear a voice from heaven declaring the Father's love for Jesus: his baptism and his transfiguration. At his baptism Jesus is in the middle of praying when a voice answers his, and as both Luke and Mark point out, it is not directed at the crowd, but to Jesus himself saying, "You are my Son, whom I love; with you I am well pleased" (Luke 3:22). This wasn't primarily for the sake of those who were witnessing his baptism. The words are directly addressed to Jesus from the Father—as Jesus was praying to the Father—and a dovelike manifestation of the Spirit was seen coming upon Jesus. Could this be a peek into the kind of prayerful, Spirit-winged conversation there was between Jesus and the Father as he developed his rhythms of life?

Later, in a private mountaintop prayer time with his three closest disciples, Peter, James and John, Jesus is joined by Moses and Elijah in a spectacular show of smoke and light. When Moses and Elijah start to leave, the disciples want to set up shelters for Jesus, Moses and Elijah, and the Father's voice is once again heard from heaven saying to all present, "This is my beloved Son, whom I have chosen, in whom I am well pleased, listen to him!" (a compilation of all three Gospel accounts). So God's declaration of his father love for Jesus, embodied by the Spirit's descent on Jesus in a dove, is a conversation with Jesus that God intends us to listen to and become involved in as participants with the Father, Son and Spirit.

As I have pondered Jesus' prayer times I have come to the conclusion that he had learned to live hearing God's voice; a constant conversation with the Father and Spirit permeated his life and ministry with love. Jesus' soul cries were met by living in this constant contact. And he needed long periods of time alone to be formed by that love, just as we do.

From this love relationship with his Father, Jesus ministered to others. From the fullness of his experience of belovedness he was able to love others who were deemed unlovable by others, even his enemies. Jesus was so full of love it spilled over to others thought unlovable—tax collectors, prostitutes, thieves and others on the margins. His interaction with an adulterous Samaritan woman at a well is a good example of how that spilled love brings life.

## THREE SOUL CRIES OF THE SOUL

There are three deep cries of the soul that Jesus answers in his time with the Samaritan woman, and I believe Jesus, as a human, found these needs met for himself in his times with the Father. Twice in the passage in John 4 we are told that she said, "Come, see a man who told me everything I ever did" (John 4:29, 39). Most commentators attribute this to the fact that the woman and John are impressed with Jesus' messianic and prophetic power to see the secrets of this woman's life. Without being told, he knew that she had multiple lovers, not just the one she was currently living with, and the villagers were impressed by this supernatural sign.

I think the true sign wasn't his supernatural knowledge but Jesus' supernatural love for her and her subsequent transformation. He knew her intimately and loved her, unlike everyone else, which healed her deepest shame. She had not experienced holy male love until she met Jesus (and his heavenly Father). And this brought about a change in her relationship with others. Now she was freed from shame to become a blessing to others. This was the greater and more impressive sign— the kind of change that took place in this formerly reclusive and shame-faced castaway.

Being known by Jesus means she was accepted and cherished, even blessed by him. Beyond the gender, ethnic and religious barriers it crossed, Jesus' request of a cup of water from the woman was sharing a basic need, placing her on an equal footing with him, in effect blessing her with purpose and meaning, which astonished and perhaps offended his disciples.

All three soul cries, *to be known* intimately, *to be cherished* and *to be blessed*, are met when we meet Jesus. Spend time in solitude as he did, to learn to hear your Father's voice.

A high school teacher showed me the Father's love and helped my soul cries be met. He took an interest in me at a time when I didn't value myself, cared enough to see potential in my writing and blessed me by helping me to develop that gift. He is the kind of teacher who is frustrated when his students aren't learning and does his utmost to enhance their education. For example, one of his classes was studying Nathaniel Hawthorne's *The Scarlet Letter* but the students were not entering into the experience the book has to offer. He tried all kinds of ways to engage them. Finally, he decided to act out the part of the adulteress on trial, putting on a dress and bonnet. He stood on his desk with someone playing the part of the judge, who was also her secret lover, condemning her. The class got into it!

My teacher's incarnational rendition of a classic book in order to engage his students is a great illustration of God's embodying his love letters, the Scriptures, in Jesus. The Father sent his Son to become one of us, a living letter to us. He led us into rhythms of learning to live in the Father's love. Prayerful meditation on those same Scriptures helped form Jesus' life and is what he still uses to form us by his Spirit in his Father's love. Jesus is our model of regularly disengaging from everyday life to be with his Father so he could engage life in the abiding presence of the Father, doing his will, listening to his voice and experiencing life in the Spirit that spills out onto others. I believe our experience of God's love for us is in direct proportion to how much time we give to being with the Father through Jesus by the Spirit, both in solitude and in service to others.

# FINDING OUR RHYTHM
## *A Day with Jesus in Luke's Gospel*

More than the other Gospel writers, Luke makes a special point of Jesus' discipline of disengaging to be alone with the Father. At first Jesus does this by himself, but then includes his disciples, "as was his custom" (Luke 4:16). These times of solitude with the Father shaped his social interactions: he engaged the crowds in the power of the Father's love. Luke has echoes of Psalm 23 in the parables of Jesus about lost sheep and sons. They reveal the Father's shepherd/host love. While the shepherd could count on the ninety-nine sheep, one high-risk sheep was lots of trouble. And both sons were lost: the prodigal, who disrespected and wasted his father's savings, and his older brother, who wasted his father's love.

Luke also tells stories about hosts. In the first, a Pharisee threw an exclusive dinner party, not welcoming tax collectors, prostitutes or lepers, those who have a place in the Father's heavenly party. Luke also describes the good Samaritan host, who went out of his way to extravagantly aid a brutally beaten Jew and even set up an account for his recuperation.

These stories see life through the belovedness Jesus experienced in solitude with his Father. He saw others through God's eyes. He saw creation and the people in it as a great banquet table set for everyone to enjoy! He looked on the crowds, sheep without a shepherd, with his Father's compassion.

Take a day away from your home or office and read *in one sitting* the whole book of Luke. Try to find a place where you can be alone for half the day, and then join others in your group to share your experience and responses to the following questions. As you read, record each time Jesus goes into solitude (to lonely places, a garden, a boat or a mountain) alone or with some of his disciples. Then list what happens when he comes back from that solitude into everyday life and ministry. Second, try to envision what Jesus may have been thinking, praying and doing in these times, keeping in mind the circumstances just before and after his time of solitude.

After reading the Scripture, see the following questions as a guide for reflection.

1. What was Jesus' practice of being with his Father like? What kind of effort did Jesus make to have it? When and where did he go? What did he do in those times?

2. What was Jesus doing immediately before and after each of these times of solitude?

3. What do these details suggest about the possible nature of Jesus' times with the Father? What might he have been praying about and reflecting on? What was he bringing to the Father?

4. How did Jesus' times with his Father help him face the demands and pressures placed on him by the crowds?

5. What does this study suggest for your own life rhythms as you face the demands and pressures of your life? In what ways could you share times of solitude with family, friends, coworkers and those you mentor?

## Sacred Space and Time: Psalm 84

How lovely is your dwelling place,
    O Lord Almighty!
My soul yearns, even faints,
    for the courts of the Lord;
my heart and my flesh cry out
    for the living God.

Even the sparrow has found a home,
    and the swallow a nest for herself,
    where she may have her young—
a place near your altar,
    O Lord Almighty, my King and my God.
Blessed are those who dwell in your house;
    they are ever praising you.

Blessed are those whose strength is in you,
    who have set their hearts on pilgrimage.
As they pass through the Valley of Baca,
    they make it a place of springs;
    the autumn rains also cover it with pools.
They go from strength to strength,
    till each appears before God in Zion.

Hear my prayer, O Lord God Almighty;
    listen to me, O God of Jacob.

Look upon our shield, O God;
    look with favor on your anointed one.

Better is one day in your courts
    than a thousand elsewhere;
I would rather be a doorkeeper in the house of my God
    than dwell in the tents of the wicked.

For the LORD God is a sun and shield;
  the LORD bestows favor and honor;
no good thing does he withhold
  from those whose walk is blameless.

O LORD Almighty,
  blessed is the man who trusts in you.

I HAVE BEEN GOING TO THE SAME retreat center for the last seventeen years. It has become a sacred space for me because God has met me there in various times of my life.

This psalm is full of references to sacred space and time. The writer is one of the sons of Korah, a family of Levites that took turns serving in the temple in Jerusalem as guards and worship leaders. When the psalmist was away from that sacred space where God was said to "touch his foot on the earth," he was jealous of the very birds that he remembered making nests in the overhangs of walls, raising their young in that atmosphere of praise and prayer.

We make each week sacred by setting aside the same day of the week for sabbath rest at church and home. We make each day sacred by starting and ending that day in the same way, giving our day to God. We make a place sacred by meeting God regularly in the same places and eventually our very bodies become saturated with God's presence, and the circumstances and events of our lives, even the painful ones, become places for God to rain blessings on us (see Psalm 84:6).

The psalmist says that those taking this time to go into sacred space are blessed by making their whole lives a pilgrimage. And their bodies become temples where God moves. Hebrew Scripture literally says that the blessing God gives those whose life is a pilgrimage is "ruts in their hearts" (Psalm 84:5), pathways of habitual walking with God so that our bodies become a place for God. The verse and psalm seem to be a foretaste of the indwelling of the Spirit in the future, where we individually and corporately become God's temple, his sacred space on earth. The psalmist longs for what we now know, because he knows also what it is to feel God's absence.

The psalm speaks of the blessedness of those who make the journey to Jerusalem during the appointed feasts and practice sacred time and space. The familiar verse, "better is one day in your courts than a thousand elsewhere" has been my meditation and has evolved for me into "better is my worst day with God than my best day without him."

- What sacred spaces and times have been significant to you?

- Where are your favorite places to pray? To retreat?

- When you think of these places, what do they evoke in you (see vv. 1-2)?

- What have you experienced from God in these places that now indwell you, a part of the fabric of your being, so that God can use you as a refuge or sacred space and time for others?

- If you are new to sacred space and time, when and where can you go to experience it on a regular basis? a private room and comfortable chair? a park bench?

# 2

# CREATING A RETREAT CENTER
# OF THE HEART

*Jesus replied, "If anyone loves me, he will obey my teaching.*
*My Father will love him, and we will come to him*
*and make our home with him."*

JOHN 14:23

*The house of my soul is too narrow for thee to come in to me;*
*let it be enlarged by thee. It is in ruins, do thou restore it.*

AUGUSTINE (354-450)

Like most of us my earliest experiences with retreat was at summer camp. My mother had packed me a week's fresh clothing for my first experience of being away from home, a second-grade summer camper. So when I got home and she opened the suitcase, she was surprised to find them still clean and neatly folded, just as she had placed them, even every clean pair of underwear and socks, a testimony to my very happy, but maybe not so clean, time there. I was so lost in being with my best friends—swimming, riding horses, weaving plastic lanyards, eating candy and drinking swamp water pop at the canteen—and having way too much fun to change my clothes.

These early camping retreats weren't for any other purpose than to just be with friends in the outdoors and, from the staff perspective, to be with God too. For my parents it was a little vacation from me. And yes, as designed and prayed for by the camp staff, I did meet Jesus and accepted him into my heart as my personal Savior. And later, to make sure he was in my life, this was followed by several rededications to "make him my Lord." (Though I now see this as disjointed, God still found fit to use it to make sacred time and space in me for him.) Even today I still feel a tug on my heart when I hear someone refer to the song we used to sing every summer: "I have decided to follow Jesus . . . no turning back, no turning back."

## ADVANCING?

Playful younger days and "being" retreats eventually gave way to highly productive "doing" retreats where as executive pastor I led and was part of team-building exercises, visioning and strategic planning, or teaching and training. These were very meaningful. I have vivid memories of staff and lay leaders with whom I strategized and planned many wonderful programs and made corporate dreams become realities.

Ultimately all this busyness was supposed to somehow serve the same goal as my early camp experiences, to help people meet and find God in the space of church programming. In some way, however, these adult retreats more often depleted me than refreshed me. And we even recognized this kind of concentrated and frenetic work by renaming them "advances." Who wants to retreat or go backward in productivity? A *retreat* seems to suggest the raising of a white flag, meaning defeat and surrender, as in losing a battle. An *advance* moves forward to the checkered flag, winning the race as we zoom ahead of the competition and become winners.

We didn't want to retreat or get away from our work. We were advancing our work, pushing the envelope of our organizational mission for more results without taking any time for retreat. This became the way I lived, advancing in doing more and more for God. It is the reason so many either burn out from the exhaustion of hyperactive ministry, fall out in sinful and self-destructive attempts to ease the pain of being a soul-shriveled but successful performer, drop out from ministry altogether for other work, or as most do, simply stumble through day after day in a zombie-like trance of joyless service to others.

But after some severe but merciful stops and hard turns, my life took a turn into "being," which eventually became the basis for my "doing." I still took time for "doing" retreats, times to get some things done. But I also began to experience a variety of "being" retreats, which produced a different kind of result. The work of these retreats was meditative reading of Scripture, centering prayer, solitude and silence, spiritual exercises and formation, listening prayer, and discernment of calling. The church staff on which I served as executive pastor began to notice and asked to go with me on my annual "Wasting Time with God" retreat, which became ours together and still is a benchmark for that church. Then I was asked to lead pastors in my seminary courses on retreats and retreat rhythms for themselves and their colleagues. I know of successful business professionals and those in the trades who have found such rhythms essential to their work being productive.

Our lives are either places of refuge and life for others or dead ends of more stress and drivenness. In our disengaging from and breaking out of the world's mold, we can become refuges. Alternatively, as we ignore our inner being and live on the surface of our lives in an endless stream of busyness, we can become stressors. Without habits of retreating into sacred space and time we will be shaped by the kind of space and time that is slowly deforming our lives. Often even our attempts at relaxing are not restorative but mere attempts to catch our breath before we once again dive into work.

## ENTERING A PLACE OF REST

Before meeting the Lord, Augustine was caught up in filling his life with all kinds of activities—pursuing pleasure, being religious and building a career in academics—that he thought would bring him peace. It wasn't until later in life that he found what he was looking for, and it came by disengaging from his pursuits and entering into sacred space and time that formed in him a place of rest, where he was found by God.

Augustine prays:

> Late have I loved Thee, O Beauty so ancient and so new. Late have I loved Thee. For behold Thou wert within me, and I outside; and I sought Thee outside, and in my unloveliness, fell upon those lovely things Thou hast made. Thou wert with me and I was not with Thee. I was kept from Thee by those things, yet had they not been in Thee, they would not have been at all.

Augustine's famous confession and prayers are evidence that he could not experience love without first going into sacred space and time to be found by God; in those spaces and times God then formed a retreat center in his heart. It is never too late for us to begin to have that same experience. Paul found it later in life as well, using spiritual disciplines as a way of avoiding the inner poverty of his soul. He disengaged for fourteen years and came out of that time full of God's love.

Paul reminds his readers that as children of God and from an inner retreat center we can participate in the prayer life of Jesus with the Father by the Spirit, where we can hear the Spirit cry, "*Abba*, Father" (Romans 8:15; Galatians 4:6). We can be deaf to this song or join in the dance with the Trinity. Jesus' prayer life, which he developed while on earth, is ours to enjoy or to drown out by turning our attention to the noise of our fears and worries.

## JESUS' INVITATION

Jesus often invited his disciples to "come away" with him. It might be to one of their homes, to a friend's place in an out-of-the-way town like Bethany, an upper room, the garden of Gethsemane, on a distant shoreline or just being in a boat on the sea. In the account of Jesus calming the storm, which appears in three of the four Gospels, Jesus is a picture of calm as he sleeps through the storm, and after he wakes he remains calm in spite of the inner storm of the disciples' fear. God has formed in him, as a result of his frequent practice of retreat, a retreat center in his heart, his body. And from that center, at the Father's side, the Spirit uses him to bring peace to those around him, and even the wind and waves calm down.

Followers of Jesus have imitated him by disengaging into sacred space and time so that they become a place for others to experience God. St. Patrick embodied the sacred presence of God, and the Celtic tradition he birthed named such spaces and times "thin places," where the distance between heaven and earth closes. These places are also called "liminal places," or openings where heaven's light and life pierces sin's shadow of death. We and our communities can be liminal or thin places where, as Paul says, we shine like stars and reflect in our faces the face of Jesus.

My son-in-law, some friends of ours and I have established a yearly rhythm in which we go to the Demontreville Ignatian Retreat House in Lake Hugo, Minnesota, to practice the Ignatian exercises. The retreat facilitators have us come during the same weekend every year, put us in the same house and the same room, and if possible allow us to sit in the same chair for the meetings. When we pray and do spiritual work in a certain spiritual space, we hallow it, sanctify it, and it forms sacred space in our spirit so that the practices, experiences and their results take hold in our body and soul as created states of new or renewed being.

Each year when it gets close to the weekend for retreat and I get that same reminder card and call to confirm my attendance, we call each other and get psyched up to go. As we arrive, put our things in that familiar room and hear the same timeless themes of truth from God's Word as translated by the life experience and exercises of Ignatius of Loyola, the fresh opportunities of the coming year and invitations of the past are met with the confidence of having already passed this way before God.

Last year's requests become this year's thanks and praises without the distraction of negotiating a new and foreign environment. In fact, praying near a statue of Joseph and Mary with baby Jesus—where the year before I had lifted up the very serious needs of my own children with tears and sobs that fell on my wooden kneeler—evoked tears again, but this time with praise for how those needs were met, which led to a fresh outpouring of requests.

Sacred space and time are not confined to the context of exercising spiritual disciplines. We experience a kind of ordinary sacred space when someone sits in Dad's or Mom's chair, or someone's place in the church pew. And there is that favorite table you frequent as much as possible in a coffee shop. It appears we were made to make certain spaces and times our own. This is why cards arrive on your birthday, for your birth on that day has made it very special. And when God is invited into these spaces and times, he makes us his home.

My son-in-law Mike's second time at the Ignatian retreat illustrates this.

The retreat comprised twelve "conferences" or meditative talks about God's loving concern for us; sin and brokenness; and the healing of seeing God in his creation, in his Son's life, death and resurrection, and in communion with others. Scripture and questions are used to pray with and ponder, and we ask God to speak to us in the time in between talks. Sacred space is enhanced through the practice of silence and the lack of chitchat and small talk of any kind. Meals are negotiated by facial and hand gestures, and everything still gets passed around. But the absence of talk keeps each person in their interior world, all in the interest of becoming disposed to hearing and seeing God with our spiritually dull eyes and ears, as the retreat introductory talk reminds us.

One of these conferences dealt with the fact that our sinful behaviors are often symptomatic of deeply wounded areas of our lives that are the soil for these sins to flourish. Heal the wound and the need for the sin may disappear. In the one hour each afternoon that we are given the option to talk with others, Mike shared the impact of the previous day's talk on him. He identified the "sin and wound" talk as a powerfully new paradigm in which to see some sins that he had a hard time with. Understanding and revisiting the wounds that might be the source of these sins, such as the hurt and pain from his parent's divorce in his early teens, brought memories of his first real crying from deep emotional pain.

The next day he reported having a vivid dream the night before. All he remembered of the dream was that he was hearing horrific and loud screams and cries of pain from someone. But contrary to the expected disturbing and nightmarish effects of having this kind of dream, he woke up with a deep and abiding sense of peacefulness and calm. Mike had just experienced the creation or re-creation of sacred space in his body, mind, heart and soul. Where pain had found a home in him, Jesus had come with the Father's love and the Spirit's touch, both in his conscious meditation and prayer and then in his subconscious.

Mike's disengagement from ordinary routine and entering sacred space and time allowed God to do his trinitarian dance of healing with Mike's spirit. As a result of God's making an internal retreat center in him, Mike can now reengage daily life and be a place of refuge for others. And these gains were secured by sharing the experience with trustworthy friends who shared in this intimate dance with God.

Mike's experience of an inner sanctuary in his heart, a retreat center that each of us are capable of developing with God's help, is what Jesus promised to his disciples when they were gathered in the upper room and reeling from the truth that he would soon die. For three years he shared his rhythms of life with them, and they had entered into a sacred space and time with him, and now it seemed to be vanishing. Jesus gave them words that they couldn't comprehend until after his resurrection: it was better that he leave them and come back to make sacred space in their very bodies as the new temple of the Trinity. Fifty days later they witnessed God's Shekinah glory as Jesus' words came true in the same manifestation of God's presence that filled the first and second temples.

When we come to know Jesus and his Spirit fills us, we begin to become the temple of God's Spirit, where the Father, Son and Spirit abide. Just as Jesus grew in his capacity for sacred space while on earth, we need to grow in the use of outer sacred space and time to cultivate and enjoy inner sacred space and time and daily communion with God.

Jesus regularly prayed in the same places, sacred spaces. He had a custom of going to lonely places in Galilee, and in Jerusalem he went often to the garden of Gethsemane. He practiced sacred time as well, observing the weekly sabbath, frequenting the synagogue and making festival trips to Jerusalem.

These sacred spaces, with their sacred times of restorative retreats and practices, are now in me, creating in my soul a retreat center I can always return to, even when lost in ministry distraction. For seventeen years my best retreat center has been my own home's back porch, with the gently flowing Crow River a few feet from my backyard, where I regularly pray or do nothing but obey Jesus' advice to waste time considering the birds and flowers. He has treated me to my own sort of National Geographic program of eagles fishing, trumpeter swans honking in flight, ospreys and hawks pursued by crows, hummingbirds sipping from flower and feeder, beavers slapping, deer leaping, and the comings and goings of red cardinals, blue jays, orange orioles, rose-breasted grosbeaks, indigo buntings and gold finches.

Due to changes in our lives and downsizing, we considered a move from our home this year, a sacred space and time which has formed our souls. My wife asked, "Keith, how are you going to get along without all this beauty—and what God does in you when you meet him there?"

After acknowledging the grief of possibly leaving it behind, I realized that due to my interior work of prayer here—the many mornings, afternoons and evenings in this sacred space and time—God had placed the beauty, peace, life and joy of being with him down deep in my heart. It could not be taken away. It was no longer dependent on that particular sacred space. God has used it to reproduce a beautiful place of retreat in my heart. That is what happens over time when practicing outer sacred space—you internalize the effects. And now you can share that inner peace, acting as a sacred space for others.

This is what I hope God's Spirit will do in you as you follow Jesus' lead in retreating to be with the Father. He will make a home in you where he his Shekinah enters your heart, which becomes a retreat center that you can share with others wherever you go. It becomes a portable refuge for God to bless others with his love.

The same is true about practicing sacred times, such as regular prayer during the day. I remember Dallas Willard, the writer whose influence started me on my journey of whole life transformation, being asked by an audience member what his morning devotional routine was. Dallas said, "Well, presently it is most days just taking a few moments to greet the Trinity upon waking and then for a few minutes, meditatively praying the twenty-third psalm and/or the Lord's Prayer, and then getting to my work for the day."

The questioner was kind of dumbfounded with the brevity of his practice and asked why it didn't involve more. Dallas explained that there are certainly times when he does more. In fact, he often takes whole days to not only pray and fast but also to practice "doing nothing," just being in creation or in simple stillness, or some activity that doesn't have a product or outcome as its goal—just being with God.

Dallas emphasized that the purpose of the spiritual disciplines wasn't to do increasingly more of them in a morning quiet time, but just enough to result in living as fully as we can in the kingdom and presence of God for the whole day. If the disciplines give us a life that reflects the fruit of the Spirit, they are doing their job. He was careful to point out that because we are never perfected in this life, we will continue to need a rhythm of disciplines, but these will change as they do their work in us. If our sacred times aren't eventually leading to make the whole day a sacred time with God, then we are missing the point of our "devotions" or "quiet time."

As we grow, discipline rhythms will need to be regularly maintained, but they will become more of the atmosphere of life, not limited to just the traditional morning quiet time. It is important to note that apprentices just starting to practice the disciplines shouldn't expect to experience the kind of life of their more experienced teachers; their teachers had to follow the same path of apprenticeship to become who and what they now are by nature. Beginning a quiet time when there was none or little before is a major accomplishment, but that time may shorten or lengthen according to our needs as we learn to be with God all through our day.

We grow as we mature in the use of the disciplines, realizing that they are not the best measure of how we are growing. The Pharisees had an extensive tithing discipline, but this discipline regimen hadn't grown them in giving mercy to widows. The disciples had intercessory prayer practices, but these didn't empower them to deal with demonic powers. The guru in one popular movie, *The Karate Kid*, affectionately calls his student "little grasshopper," similar to Jesus calling his disciples of "little faith" because their practices failed to empower them for life's storms. Jesus' prayer life had the power of a few words, "Peace, be still."

One of the marks of those who teach on spiritual disciplines and know them deeply is that their everyday life and demeanor exude other-centered humility, calming gentleness, deep listening and obedient authority. Beyond just being routines or practices, these fruits of the Spirit become the atmosphere of their lives. Often you will hear from those who have been with them say, "I bet that was what it felt like to be in the presence of Jesus." You want their life, not just their routines.

# Finding Our Rhythm
## *Storm on the Sea* Icon

Plan on getting to some sacred space for a couple of hours, a place where God has often met you—that same chair, outdoor place or retreat center. Be sure that this is not a time when you will have to rush from something or to something, or where you can be easily distracted. Or plan a day or half-day retreat with your group using the following exercise.

Read Mark 4:35-41. Then read it a second time, but before reading place yourself in the boat with the disciples, becoming one of them as you read. Answer the following questions:

1. Why do you think Jesus was so tired that he could sleep peacefully during a storm? List as many reasons as you can. Note that Jesus was whisked away into the boat and other boats were following him. Does this remind you of a Hollywood star being pursued by paparazzi? What clues do you get from this Scripture or from what you know about Jesus' ministry, life and human nature that might make you think so?

Jesus was so busy that he had to use a boat as his office. What did sacred spaces like this do for him? Why was it important for Jesus to have such sacred spaces and times in his life?

Dallas Willard believes that Jesus' rebuke wasn't because the disciples didn't see him as God and unable to do a miracle, but that they were afraid of dying and lacked the confidence that they would be with their Father in heaven. Jesus saw the universe as God's pasture for him, all of this world held in his hand as sacred space, every event as sacred time, and although in this world we will have storms that rock our boat, we have a peace available from God in us that can give us peace in our worst circumstances—even facing death itself.

2. Look at the icon of *Storm on the Sea* and answer these questions:

This icon illustrates the peaceful space in Jesus. Icons are helps to prayer that have been used in the church both East and West. They are not meant to be realistic portraits but point away from themselves to the spiritual realities they portray. In this one the two disciples in the boat with Jesus represent our two basic responses to the storms in our life: flight (John) and fight (Peter). Jesus offers a third response: rest in God. What might the iconographer have meant to convey by the postures and gestures of the three figures? What emotions or attitudes do you sense the posture and gesture of each figure is conveying? Peter (standing up)? John (sitting down)? Jesus (sleeping)?

Ponder the icon prayerfully and reflect on your life during the last few weeks or months. What winds and waves are rocking and threatening the boat of your life—family, school, friends or work?

What do you worry about or fear (Peter's worried, fearful pleading)?

What gets you down or causes you to be numb or stuck (John's resigned and depressed look and posture)?

The world of peace is possible for you—the place of rest and trust that is with Jesus. Where would you have him speak, "Peace, be still" into your life?

Note that the wind is whipping Peter's coat to form what looks like wings. And that both Peter and John have halos. In his flight into despair, John isn't looking directly at Jesus, but he still is glancing at his master out of the corner of his eye. The icon suggests transformation is possible when we bring our disordered being to Jesus. Then we can begin to live in Jesus' end of the boat—in peace and confidence and rest in God's care, even as we face death. And we can come just as we are, full of fear or weakened by depression.

To bring more of this peace into your life, play a favorite song that brings you peace or a sense of God's unfailing presence. When the song is done, imagine yourself hearing and receiving Jesus' words "Peace, be still" in your life and circumstances. I use two songs from Steven Curtis Chapman: "Be Still and Know" along with the instrumental piece just before it, "The Journey." "The Journey" starts with gentle rolling measures and crescendos that remind me of a sudden storm. During this, I lift up to God all the storms threatening my life, pushing me to anxious fight or despairing flight. Then, when the music ends abruptly, I say aloud "Peace, be still" over the things I have lifted up to God. Then I rest in the peace of the next song, imagining myself close to the Father's side, in complete trust and peace.

## Wilderness Living: Psalm 63

O God, you are my God,
    earnestly I seek you;
my soul thirsts for you,
    my body longs for you,
in a dry and weary land
    where there is no water.

I have seen you in the sanctuary
    and beheld your power and your glory.
Because your love is better than life,
    my lips will glorify you.
I will praise you as long as I live,
    and in your name I will lift up my hands.
My soul will be satisfied as with the richest of foods;
    with singing lips my mouth will praise you.

On my bed I remember you;
    I think of you through the watches of the night.
Because you are my help,
    I sing in the shadow of your wings.
My soul clings to you;
    your right hand upholds me.

They who seek my life will be destroyed;
    they will go down to the depths of the earth.
They will be given over to the sword
    and become food for jackals.

But the king will rejoice in God;
    all who swear by God's name will praise him,
while the mouths of liars will be silenced.

I HAVE NEVER LIVED IN A DESERT but have felt spiritually dry and depleted many times. Sometimes it is due to circumstances—when friends have let me down or I feel God has deserted me. At other times I just don't feel close to God and for no apparent reason he seems far away. When this happens, I turn to this psalm to lament and cry out to God for his touch.

Psalm 63 is described as a psalm of David and was probably written on the occasion of his being in the desert of Judah. David was familiar with deserts and wildernesses, where he worked as the family shepherd and learned to sling stones at lions and bears to protect sheep. David later spent time in hiding in the desert before he was king and after he had reigned for some time. The first time was when he was being chased by the mercurial Saul, who was suspect of David's loyalty and jealous of his anointing by Samuel. David hid from Saul in caves and desolate places. While David was king, his son Absalom led a coup and a civil war broke out, forcing David to flee once more to the desert.

Our life circumstances can become deserts for us. When we are being hassled and mistreated by others, or even betrayed and abandoned, we experience some of the most dry and painful times of our lives. Failures and disappointments take on the nature of caves and prisons with no escape. When we encounter these and invite God into these trying times and places, we can find a fresh experience of God's grace and deliverance. The desert can become a place of great growth, and our fear can turn into an expectation of transformation whenever we find ourselves there.

King David and others like Anthony of Egypt found God in desolation and deprivation. Indeed, David said, he was able to "sing in the shadow of [his] wings" (Psalm 63:7).

Night too can be a desert experience for us. This time of supposed replenishment can be full of nightmares and insomnia. One of David's practices was to "remember and think of God through the watches of the night." He seems to turn his sleeplessness into an opportunity to dwell on God's character and promises proven in the past. He had a library of memories of how God had come through for him in the end. He puts himself to sleep, counting his blessings and resting in God's care (Psalm 63:6).

- Times of betrayal, misunderstanding or conflict can often be desert places in our lives. Loss of various kinds can also leave us dry, weary and utterly alone. How do you relate to desert experiences?

- What do you find difficult and wearying about these times?

- What longings cry out from your places of pain as you try to seek God in these times?

- What delivering acts of God are you currently in need of? As you suffer, what life-threatening voices and messages need to be cut off, silenced and buried by God?

- How has God met you in the desert experiences of your past?

# ENCOUNTERING THE
# ANCIENT DESERT
# AND POSTMODERN WILD

*And the Spirit immediately drove him out into the wilderness.*
*He was in the wilderness forty days, tempted by Satan; and he was*
*with the wild beasts; and the angels waited on him.*

MARK 1:12-13 (NRSV)

*If you want to, you can become all flame.*

JOSEPH OF PANEPHYSIS

*O*ur environments shape who we are and how we experience life. Increasingly, our experience of life is suburbs and cities where God's creation is transformed into paved streets, parking lots and buildings. Many have never seen a starry night or been to a forest inhabited by wild creatures reflecting God's glory. A re-creative force works in us when we spend time in God's creation versus being in fabricated space.

I grew up in suburbia—different versions of the same basic Midwestern tract housing on small patches of lawn circumscribed by asphalt streets and concrete curbs. So when my wife, who grew up on a farm, realized we had the opportunity to move to a small hobby farm, she was delighted. I wasn't, at first. I wasn't used to driving more than a half hour to work or to a movie, a shopping mall or a decent restaurant. But after a while it grew on me. I slowed down as I drove by fields and forest, watching for wildlife. Our kids loved it.

We were able to have some chickens, a few horses and even a cow. Along with my daughter and son I learned from my wife how to feed and care for these animals. When we bought a young bull for my daughter Cara to raise, I was told by the farmer who sold it that I needed to watch out because more farmers were killed by charging bulls than from tractor or machinery accidents. I didn't see how, "Clarence," this cute little three-week-old, bottle-fed calf would be a threat to me. Then one day, a few months later, I turned around to see all one thousand pounds of lovable Clarence charging at me.

I remembered the farmer telling me that if I was too close when Clarence charged, the best thing I could do was stand my ground and punch him on the nose. It wouldn't hurt him, but he would stop. So when I belted Clarence, the next thing I heard was Cara screaming as she charged me and pummeled my back. She forgave me once she understood why I had hit her pet.

On the hobby farm, biblical images from an agricultural world started to take on new meaning for me, and when a psalm mentions God as our horn (a bull's, not a bugle) and strength, I flash back to my almost being trampled by Clarence. It makes sense now.

Other biblical images came alive. When Cara's favorite chicken hatched her chicks, she was thrilled, picking them up and holding them in her hand. But one day the chicks disappeared and Cara was distraught. Where were they? Had they been eaten by a predator? My wife came to the rescue. She told Cara to gently lift the mother hen's trembling wing. Underneath the shelter of that wing we found all the chicks, chirping in delight.

## THE DESERT

Rural life also familiarized me with how Jesus and others made use of the desert, a place where dependency on God is strongest.

Out in the country, at night, I experience the absence of human sounds and sights that can only come from being far removed from others. David declares, "Because you are my help, I sing in the shadow of your wings" (Psalm 63:7). But he isn't on a pleasant hobby farm. He is in another environment unfamiliar to most of us, a desert. I have never been too fond of the desert. My first desert experience was as a kid traveling through Arizona for a few days during a 100-degree summer in a camper with the air conditioner broken. My dad bought us a bag of ice to suck on. Perhaps David found refuge in the cool of a cave.

It appears that God does some of his best work in deserted places. Places where we think God will be hard to find, David and others made into springs of life that watered their souls, so they could sing in the cool of God's presence.

Jesus was familiar with the desert. Luke tells us that Jesus had a custom of going to lonely or deserted places, and one of them was the desert (Luke 4:42; 5:16). Not many people are in deserts. They are harsh, dry and hot. They often harbor animals we wouldn't want to meet up with—such as the jackals or wild dogs David mentions in Psalm 63. But that is why deserts have been an environment of formation for many. Moses shepherded both sheep and the people of Israel in the Sinai desert. John the Baptist lived in the desert, wearing a camel hair coat and eating wild honey and locusts. Paul spent years in the desert of Arabia. And the desert became a training ground for third-century desert fathers and mothers, influencing monastics through church history.

After Jesus was baptized and we overhear the Father's loving communication with Jesus, Jesus is *hurled* (Greek word *ekballo* in Mark 1:12) into the desert by the Spirit. The other Gospels say he was *led* by the Spirit, which I take to mean that this was not against Jesus' will but was a place of preparation and formation that was part of Jesus' regular pattern of life, taking lengthy times of solitude and silence in the company of animals and angels. This is unusual to us, but in the history of the church the desert has been the place where saints fled to prepare to stand life in the wilds of the world and culture.

## STANDING AGAINST THE WILD OF THE WORLD

Athanasius writes of one of these monastics, Antony of the Desert, who kept going deeper into the wilderness due to all the people coming to learn from him. Antony was followed by thousands who became known as the desert fathers and mothers. Some surely were selfish and self-occupied in their flight from society. But the example of the devout influenced Benedict and others who, instead of fleeing to the desert, created monastic communities to cultivate a place of witness to the world of a different kind of life.

Today there is a new wave of monastic influence among younger Christians of differing traditions. They relocate to the margins of society, the desert of the city, the inner city, places of poverty and urban blight. They seek to recapture a missional life that is largely and increasingly lost to ordinary church life. The church, they believe, is being molded by the world.

We live in a postmodern "wild" that gives us a false sense of what truly brings life. Technology provides increasing opportunities to communicate by cell phones, tablets and multimedia, all conveniently held in our hands. Some believe these will be reduced to a chip in our heads. Thus technology will allow us to virtually "live in our heads," an ironic and empty imitation of the kind of retreat center God offers us in our hearts.

Our connectivity through social networks and electronic gadgets distance us from the real space and time required to have true and deep relationships. In this new postmodern wild we are connected but lonelier than ever. This is illustrated by the fact that the highest use of and money made on the Internet is through pornography, which dehumanizes the viewer, the viewed and view purveyors.

We have more and more to possess in terms of cars, houses and toys; we have everything we want but are often unaware how poor we really are in spirit and soul. The evidence of this poverty is our longing for the "real, organic and natural" as opposed to the manufactured imitation of God's creation.

This postmodern wild is marketed to us by Madison Avenue, purchased from Wall Street and Hollywood, and leveraged by bailouts from Washington. It creates a noisy life of mostly meaningless chatter and useless information. It is easy to get caught up in this chase after meaning and a bigger-faster-stronger life. Ultimately it benefits few. In reality, the life we seek will be ours only through a painful resizing, slowing down and admitting our weakness. Then we start allowing God to mysteriously redeem us as we cooperate with him to create rhythms of sacred space and time in our bodies, which will usher in a new world for us, the kingdom of heaven. To do this we must submit to entering some kind of retreat or desert, or in a severe mercy we might wind up there against our will—for our good.

*Into the Wild* is the true story of Christopher McCandless, who upon graduating with distinction from college had plenty of money saved for graduate school. But he gave it away to charity and then left his family without any forwarding address. He also left his identity by burning his various forms of identification and renaming himself Alexander Supertramp. After a cross-country pilgrimage that confirmed his view of America's cultural poverty, he left society for a life alone in the wild, deep in Alaska, subsisting on what he could hunt or gather. He took his favorite books along, Thoreau's *Walden* and a book on surviving in the wild.

After a first exhilarating season, having found shelter in a rundown and abandoned bus, he journals about entering the deserted wilderness to find peace. We don't know how his journey actually ends, or whether he reaches his goal of inner peace, because he dies in the wilderness. But according to the film Christopher found peace, because he refers to God's blessing in his life and writes his given name once more to identify himself to those who find his journal and body.

My adult children and their friends formed a kind of cult following of this film, watching it over and over and listening to the haunting soundtrack, because it expresses their desire to somehow escape the postmodern wild for a different kind of life than the American Dream.

## CONFRONTING THE WILD WITHIN

There are many reasons why people have journeyed to the desert. One of the most common is that the desert has a way of helping us confront our self-deception and know the truth about ourselves, both our sin and our potential for God's life in us. Although those who went into the desert did so to escape the "world," they knew that there was a greater wild within themselves that the solitude and stress of the desert would expose.

Jesus' forty-day temptation in the desert prepared him for the temptations in the everyday world. The desert fashioned a strong internal place of retreat within him. He was being formed when he turned down Satan's three attempts to pervert his ministry. Later, when Jesus was pressured by the crowd to assume the role of a king, he tapped into an inner retreat center formed while in the desert. The desert is where we reduce our outer distractions to face the more powerful distractions in our hearts and minds.

There is a story from the desert fathers of a visit one father made to another to ask how he was doing at his devotional practices. Abba Lot went to see Abba Joseph and said to him, "Abba, as far as I can, I say my little office, I fast a little, I pray and meditate, I live in peace, and as far as I can, I purify my thoughts. What else can I do?"

Then Abba Joseph stood up and stretched his hands toward heaven. His fingers became like ten lamps of fire and he said to him, "If you want to, you can become all flame." The desert is not a place to fine-tune our devotional habits, it is a place where we are stripped of everything pretentious to get to the reality of who we are and what we can become. We reach our full potential—becoming "all flame." And sometimes we don't get to pick our time in the desert, it comes as a fiery trial without our asking. Like Jesus, we too are sometimes "hurled" into the desert for refining.

Our son Kyle went through a period when he was making lots of money and began to live the high life, partying hard, changing his friends and habits, and God was all but forgotten. His mother and I began to feel what it was like to have a son lost in a far away country, like the father of the prodigal son. His high life all began to come tumbling down when he was ticketed driving while intoxicated in a city where the penalties were harsh. Even a first-time offense included a stiff penalty and three days and four nights in jail.

We will never forget taking him to serve that time. While waiting with Kyle for his processing to serve his jail time, we saw angry and tough-looking men and women, some cursing as they went in and out, and I saw the anxiety and fear on Kyle's face. All the stories of what prison might be like were playing in our minds. Next to Kyle was a young man who was going to be in this county jail for a whole year. He would become Kyle's cellmate.

During those three days, we prayed that God would protect Kyle's heart and mind, and that a genuine repentance would start to take hold—that his lukewarm heart for God would be "all flame." And it did. But we didn't expect it to begin right there in that jail cell. While in jail, Kyle's attention was centered on the condition of his inner life. He had time to ponder the root causes of his pursuit of the high life and how they were driving him to live recklessly, immune to the consequences of his patterns of life.

His Latino cellmate became his friend. Playing cards at first, Kyle decided to read whatever books were available at the jail. There was only a Spanish Bible, so he asked his roommate if he would read and translate some psalms. One psalm I had shared with Kyle, Psalm 107, spoke of those in prison who cried out to God in their pain and were released, and also found new life in God's unfailing love.

Kyle's new friend was comforted by the psalms he was reading to Kyle. He told Kyle that in all the time he went to church as a boy he had never read a Bible and was surprised at psalms written for those in prison. Kyle told him that many of the psalms were cries of pain from people in caves, deserts and tough spots who found God's presence and peace in their hearts, even though their circumstances weren't yet changed. As Kyle left on the last day, he promised to pray for his friend and urged him to keep reading the psalms during the year he had left in the cell.

It was the beginning of God's work of creating a retreat center in Kyle's life. While God had been largely on the outside of Kyle's life, with occasional times of intimacy when he was younger, God was now becoming his constant companion. Subsequently Kyle volunteered to thirty days of treatment. When his health provider suggested outpatient treatment, Kyle argued that he wanted to really deal with his problem, and he won over the provider to fund treatment. When finished he checked into a sober house, lived there for almost a year and now has a habit of going to several AA meetings a week and giving his life in service to others.

Kyle found God in the cell of a prison, treatment center, sober house and now his meetings. But this is not a begrudging new life; he has found community and service in helping others find peace with God within the sacred space and time of their hearts. But that requires making some sacred time and space in their outer lives.

I now believe that God does his best work in caves, cells and deserts, whether monasteries, retreat centers or prisons. Whether we are forced to be in one or choose to submit ourselves, God transforms these into sacred space and time to make room for the Trinity to dwell in us.

# Finding Our Rhythm
## Watching *Into the Wild*

Take an evening with your family or friends and watch the film *Into the Wild*, which is available through Netflix and Amazon. My children have a number of movies that they watch repeatedly. But by far the one they return to most often is *Into the Wild*. They have a strange fascination with Christopher's in-your-face rejection of our culture's restless pursuit of the American Dream and his courage to find solitude and peace on his own, in the wilderness.

Try to watch the film with a variety of age groups: teenagers, twenty- or thirty-somethings, baby boomers and older folks. Notice how similarly or differently these three groups react to the film. Note that there are some scenes that are not suitable for children.

After viewing the film, reflect on these questions:

1. What elements of the world's "wild" did Christopher experience that fueled his exit into the wilderness of Alaska?

2. How do you relate—or not—to Alexander Supertramp's assessment of society and his desire to drop out? Is that attractive to you? Why?

3. Have you ever thought of joining a monastery or closed community of some kind? How do you think you would be in that setting?

4. How can you find those same things by pursuing more sacred space and time in your life?

5. What are the forces in our society that have shaped you, your family and your friends?

6. What effect has our increased information access and the pursuit of possessions, pleasure and "living large" had on you, your family and your friends?

7. How have you or might you find your own sacred places and times that can function like the desert to orient you toward the reality and blessing of God's life, his kingdom dream for you and your world?

## Divine Constant Contact: Psalm 139

O LORD, you have searched me
    and you know me.
You know when I sit and when I rise;
    you perceive my thoughts from afar.
You discern my going out and my lying down;
    you are familiar with all my ways.
Before a word is on my tongue
    you know it completely, O LORD.

You hem me in—behind and before;
    you have laid your hand upon me.
Such knowledge is too wonderful for me,
    too lofty for me to attain.

Where can I go from your Spirit?
    Where can I flee from your presence?
If I go up to the heavens, you are there;
    if I make my bed in the depths, you are there.
If I rise on the wings of the dawn,
    if I settle on the far side of the sea,
even there your hand will guide me,
    your right hand will hold me fast.

If I say, "Surely the darkness will hide me
    and the light become night around me,"
even the darkness will not be dark to you;
    the night will shine like the day,
    for darkness is as light to you.

For you created my inmost being;
    you knit me together in my mother's womb.
I praise you because I am fearfully and wonderfully made;

your works are wonderful,
    I know that full well.
My frame was not hidden from you
    when I was made in the secret place.
When I was woven together in the depths of the earth,
    your eyes saw my unformed body.
All the days ordained for me
    were written in your book
    before one of them came to be.

How precious to me are your thoughts, O God!
    How vast is the sum of them!
Were I to count them,
    they would outnumber the grains of sand.
When I awake,
    I am still with you.

If only you would slay the wicked, O God!
    Away from me, you bloodthirsty men!
They speak of you with evil intent;
    your adversaries misuse your name.
Do I not hate those who hate you, O LORD,
    and abhor those who rise up against you?
I have nothing but hatred for them;
    I count them my enemies.

Search me, O God, and know my heart;
    test me and know my anxious thoughts.
See if there is any offensive way in me,
    and lead me in the way everlasting.

THIS PSALM DEMONSTRATES a consciousness of God that anyone can access if they train their attention to do so. The psalmist's life is drenched with God, both before he was conscious of God—who has knit him together by hand—and by coming to take that hand grasping him and drawing him into a close relationship, so close that God's face is the first thing he sees upon waking up and the last thought in the dark of night. The notion of being nearby or being held by God's right hand is one that David uses frequently to describe God's palpable presence in his life. In Psalm 16 it is his assurance that even when put in the grave his body will not be forsaken but will be kept by God. His entire life, from beginning to end, is enveloped by God.

I love that God is simply with David, watching over him. I believe that this kind of silent partnering is what God does most for us. He doesn't want to be like the chattering person you get stuck with on an airplane. He is more like a best friend or loved one who is at ease with us, satisfied to be in our presence and available to us. Those speaking in this psalm are David and God's enemies, who are far from God and whom David wants far from him. They use God's name for their selfish purposes. David wishes they were silenced. In response, he asks God to test his life—his thoughts and words and ways.

- Have you experienced the kind of closeness with God David writes about here? When did you first notice God's presence? How old were you? Describe it.

- As you read this psalm, list the ways God knows you. What does he know of your past, your present, your future, your outer circumstances, your inner life?

- David asks God to search him for anxious thoughts. As you ask God to search you, what are you anxious about?

- What do you think your anxiety (or worry about your life) has to do with things you do that are offensive to yourself, others and God? What ways would your offensive behavior be less so if you were more peaceful and aware of God's care?

# 4

## GOING OFF-LINE

*At that time Jesus, full of joy through the Holy Spirit, said,*
*"I praise you Father, Lord of heaven and earth, because you have hidden these*
*things from the wise and learned, and revealed them to little children.*
*Yes, Father, for this was your good pleasure."*

LUKE 10:21

*We may ignore, but we can nowhere evade, the presence of God.*
*The world is crowded with Him. He walks everywhere incognito. And the*
*incognito is not always easy to penetrate. The real labor is to remember to attend.*
*In fact to come awake. Still more to remain awake.*

C. S. LEWIS

$\mathcal{I}$ have resisted getting the latest phone applications that can access the Internet. Why? I don't want to be that plugged in. And it isn't due to my being so spiritually disciplined that I am fasting from technology. My problem is how hooked I am right now with the cell phone in my pocket, my laptop's easy portability and the wireless service at home for Internet surfing, iTunes browsing, being on Facebook and checking Gmail.

I don't want to join the growing number of those enslaved to their

gadgets. Have you heard the reports of accidents involving those text-
ing while driving or walking? Studies are being done that document
the damage done to children whose parents are so wired and increasingly withdrawn that they are less available to their children's needs.
It is time to count the cost of our advances in technology and our ability to access one another and information.

My lack of desire for the latest tech offering isn't because I am
against all these wonderful inventions. I am grateful to be writing this
book on my Mac laptop and being able to store and then send manu-
scripts to the publisher by e-mail. I also check out other books on the
Internet. These technologies are changing our world for the better.
Look, for example, at the effect it has had on repressive governments
during the Arab Spring of 2011. I enjoy being able to communicate via
Facebook with students I have taught in China, Nepal and Uganda.
These are powerful gifts. But to be able to use and not be used by
these devices we need to have more power in our bodies and character
to be able to put them down or unplug them for a while.

I have colleagues and friends who refuse to adapt to various parts of
the wired lifestyle because they have practiced a kind of lifelong fast
from certain aspects of technological advance. One friend doesn't
carry a cell phone. So when he needs to be picked up at an airport he
is just fine with waiting to get to a land line if his plane is late; in fact,
he has turned all his unanticipated waiting into random and welcome
times to be with God, singing a hymn softly to himself or meditating
on a passage of Scripture or just doing nothing but waiting.

Another friend has carefully crafted a life of stability and simplicity
in subsistence farming and ranching, and does use a cell phone occasionally but only when he travels. He has taken the unusual step of not
having e-mail, although he uses browses and downloads books on his
Kindle. I have to snail mail him or catch him on his land line when he
is at home. And there is no answering machine. These friends have
found that losses accompany our gains in applying more and more

technology to our lives. Thus they selectively use technology so that it serves, rather than enslaves, them to it.

The other day I found a bunch of cassette tapes on which I had recorded classic rock albums, collected in what I think of as the golden age of rock—the late sixties and early seventies. I would tape my vinyls to keep the scratchless sound when they were new. But after buying my iPod, I threw the tapes out, because I no longer had a tape player and knew they wouldn't match the clearer sound of my iPod anyway.

But it is intriguing that renewed interest is stirring in those black vinyl discs, which apparently provide more of a "live" studio sound. The highly compressed MP3 files flatten out the sound when compared to vinyl's full feast of sound, especially for those who love the layered and nuanced orchestral sounds of classical music.

Yet it is so easy now to access all my tunes in one digitalized space. I have stored enough music on my computer so that I won't hear the same song twice even if listening 24/7 for sixty days. The days of removing vinyl records from album jackets, placing them under a turntable's spindle and then recording my own mix on a tape recorder seem like ages ago. Yet in the time saved, it seems that something has been lost, and we are somehow poorer for all the advances. Unless we are called to live in a version of monastic technological poverty or an Amish abstinence from development, how will most of us keep from being formed in the "cell" of our phones or reducing our relational connections to our virtual but basically unknown friends to tweets and tags?

This was reinforced for me the other day when in a panicked rush out of the house I left my computer, my iPod and cell phone behind. When I discovered this I was too far away to retrieve them. For tunes the radio had to suffice, and due to my schedule I would have to wait ten hours until I could check my e-mail, Facebook or favorite websites. But the biggest effect of my unintended technology fast was being without my cell phone. About halfway through the day I noticed that I was constantly reaching to check my cell phone. I was wired to use that device in a way I would never have known apart from having forgotten it.

This gave me insight into why I found it harder to practice God's presence after my time of morning prayer. It made me wonder if there was so much more of God's presence and partnering that I could find if I was more unplugged, off-line and cell-less. It made me examine my life to see if I had lost an openness to God carefully cultivated by past practices.

I was a bit surprised at this wiring of mine, since I found it easy to be on the technology-free retreats I teach and lead for schools and churches. The students discover how hard-wired they are to their electronic devices when they are not allowed to use them for a weekend, but even more so for an entire week. One student had severe anxiety attacks due to not being able to check in with her family and friends by phone or e-mail.

She found it impossible to be present to the exercises of prayer and quiet because these highlighted her need for human contact. She passed the course, having toughed it out and filling the requirements, but she didn't evidence the same transformation the others did, passing from the dis-ease of technological deprivation to the peace of being more present to God and others.

## UNPLUGGED, OFF-LINE AND CELL-FREE

Being at the Ignatian retreat center, which I mentioned earlier in the book, in the freedom of the unplugged, off-line and cell-free space and time, is a good reminder of what we may be losing by being so well "connected." Without critically examining the tsunami of technological devices now forming us to think we are more connected and productive, we may be deceived. We actually are becoming more isolated and stunted in our relational worlds, our souls being rewired for a virtual, but not the real, world.

Just up the hill from the Ignatian retreat center are men's and women's Carmelite monasteries that are open for a few hours each day to visitors. They are partially funded by selling items to the retreatants who wander up the hill and onto their gated grounds. The women are cloistered and cannot be seen. There is no contact except for what is allowed in a little entryway that has a speaker box on the wall for sharing concerns with a sister behind the wall. There is also a revolving compartment in which to trade written prayer requests or donations for a prayer card or to purchase a rosary. I have placed my most longed for and serious requests in these sisters' hands, knowing that they will be prayed for by those whose sole vocation is to live for prayer. Their whole life is orientated to help them stay attentive to God and intercession. This reminds retreatants that they have entered an area that is detached from the world's distractions and busyness.

The men are not cloistered but live in a complex of cells for each monk and public rooms where they eat, work or worship. When someone knocks on the monastery door, one of the monks will let the person into the bookstore and answer any questions or even schedule a time for prayer and spiritual counsel. On one visit one of my friends asked Father Daniel how he had been led to enter the monastery. Besides the founding abbot, Daniel was one of the first to come to the monastery to give spiritual guidance and leadership to the Carmelite sisters next door.

He came at the age of eighteen and had now been there for five years, having gone through a discernment and trial period of three years before being accepted as a full member under vows. Before becoming a monk, he had been discouraged when he tried to witness to his faith, finding more often than not that his words bounced off those he shared with. So after being introduced to the Carmelite order and the life of intercession they led for others and the world, he felt he could make more of an impact on others through a life of ordered and constant prayer.

Later, my friend and I shared how surprised we were that the Carmelites' undistracted lives weren't given to being alone with God as some kind of escape from others or the world; they were there to devote themselves to praying and engaging the world in ways they were not able to when in the world. Their obvious hospitality to us, their attention to our needs and the story they told of their prayer life for others blew up our preconceived notions that they were out of touch with reality. Perhaps, we conjectured, we are the ones distracted, out of reality due to the isolation of modern life.

We learned that nothing happened quickly at the monasteries and the pace was peaceful. Our little group of four probably disturbed the tranquility by our rather loud and sometimes raucous talk while walking up to their living quarters and bookstore. But the brothers who greeted our noisy group didn't show any annoyance. After a day and a half of quiet during our four days of practicing silence, we were glad to talk during this break. We were easily distracted from the goal of being quiet before God and each other. The retreat director had predicted this but hoped we would desist from talk that distracted our attention from God and come to value what he called "becoming disposed" to hear God.

One person in our group was looking at a little book on prayer by a Carmelite master that dealt with distractions and prayer, and he asked Father Daniel what the book said. He told us a story to illustrate the work needed to become focused and undisturbed in prayer. Once when Saint Bernard of Clairvaux was traveling from his monastery, he came upon a monk who asked Bernard about his prayer practice and what he had learned over the years. Bernard shared how many years he had been working on being less distracted by his cares and worries, and was just beginning to feel some degree of peace. But he still struggled with distractions. At this the monk began to boast about his progress in prayer and how undistracted he now was.

Bernard proposed a test to see what there was to learn from this

monk who claimed to pray so well at so young an age. He suggested
that they see if the monk could pray the "Our Father" without being
distracted. And to make the test have some teeth he offered the monk
his horse if he could pray one "Our Father" without being distracted.
So the monk took him up on this offer and began to pray, saying, "Our
Father, who art in heaven, hallowed be thy name." Then he stopped
and asked Bernard if he could have the saddle too.

We all laughed at this monastic humor, and I wondered if the story
was true or a legend. But as the week went on I began to notice how
inattentive I was and unable to focus in prayer. I wasn't preoccupied
with acquiring saddles and horses, but had often wandered from the
meditation and prayer exercises we were to use for the time between
sessions, worrying about my car brakes or a tire that seemed to be
flat, which might indicate the need for new ones. And those thoughts
led to the fact that I had just spent my spare money to fix the icemaker
in the fridge.

And the cell phone that I hoped to keep in the car during the retreat (so I wouldn't use it) made its way up to my room. And I was
taking walks to the farthest edges of the retreat center late at night to
get and return my messages. My first book had just been printed, and
I was anxious to know if those free copies had arrived. I knew I was
not able to read them while on retreat, but my curiosity and excite-
ment over the book had a power over me that I couldn't resist.

Just as I was heading back to my room I came upon one of my friends
and he saw the cell phone. He just shook his head and laughed. Here I
was, the one who had invited my friends to try some time off-line, detached and unhooked, and I was finding out how distracted I really
was.

So I am trying to come up with ways to keep my electronic devices
my servants rather than me being their slave. My son-in-law occasionally goes on what he calls a technology fast, not when in social settings
but when he is alone for a whole day. Perhaps this exercise would be a

good one for us to practice in combination with a sabbath day. And our time at the retreat center and the monasteries taught us the purpose of such exercises and disciplines. The priests and monks were not against technology. In fact they used it in moderation to do some of their work.

# FINDING OUR RHYTHM
## *Praying Your Day*

You and your group can practice these three forms of drawing near to and being with God for a few days or even a week, and notice if you are "becoming more disposed" to experience God's and others' presence. Keep a journal to record how these four exercises affect your experience of daily life and whether they open you up more to live more reflectively and in the moment with God, others and yourself.

1. Before you go to bed, let your last thought be a prayer to God committing yourself and others to him. Use Phyllis Tickle's adaptation of this evening prayer: "Into your hands, O Lord, I commend my spirit; for you have redeemed me, O Lord, O God of truth. Keep me, O Lord, as the apple of your eye; hide me under the shadow of your wings." Ask God to wake you up in the morning, and after greeting him, pray this prayer.

2. Set aside some time in the morning to pray your day's schedule. Examine what people you will meet or activities you will participate in. Bring each person or activity to God for his blessing and invite his presence into that time or event. See what fears or hopes come to mind as you think of the day's activities, and bring those to God as requests or thanksgivings. Then, as you go through your

day and meet these people or engage in these activities, stop before each one and invite God again, bringing a request or thanks as well.

3. Before you retire at night, review the day, meditating on and answering these two questions: What am I grateful for today and can thank God for? What am I not grateful for this past day and need to bring to God?

4. Take two or even three days, maybe over a weekend, to experience how it is to be totally without your electronic gadgets and the virtual world. Unplug yourself from all forms of technology, including the radio or iPod in the car. Go without cable or satellite TV, stay off-line and off your computer, and don't allow your phone to be anywhere near you, not just turned off. Notice how often you instinctively reach for the phone or feel the nudge to check your e-mail or your social network site. Notice how tied you are to being plugged in.

When you have the urge to pick up the phone and make a call, or tweet something, or get on the computer, or watch TV, transform that urge into prayer. Replace communication with others with some form of communion with God. Repeat a verse or section of verses. Sing a favorite song or hymn to God in your heart. Or lift up someone's needs in prayer, or simply bless them.

## Soul Shushing: Psalm 131

My heart is not proud, O LORD,
　my eyes are not haughty;
I do not concern myself with great matters
　or things too wonderful for me.
But I have stilled and quieted my soul;
　like a weaned child with its mother,
　like a weaned child is my soul within me.

O Israel, put your hope in the LORD
　both now and forevermore.

THIS PSALM OF DAVID is one of my favorites because it shows us the
feminine side of God, nurturing and being there as a presence to lean
on and rest against. It also shows a gentle and childlike side of a powerful king who assumes the posture of a child with God as a sign of
trust. There are no plans or schemes of what he will do for God, or
what God can do for him; just being with God is enough. It goes
against our Western idolatry of productivity and our worship of a
God who often is an idol of our making, one who helps us get what
we want done, often at the expense of relationships with others and
God himself.

The child is pictured as a newly weaned child, which in that ancient
culture could have been anywhere from two to five years old. The
weaned child no longer goes to the mother for food but merely for the
mother's presence. David says he has quieted or stilled his soul. Mothers often shush their babies as a gentle way of helping them stop crying
or calm down. Some have speculated that this universal phenomenon
among moms is soothing and comforting to babies because it is similar
to what babies heard in the womb. The "shhhhhuuuusssh" sound is
loud enough to drown out crying or chatter, but quiet enough to lead
to a peaceful state of being. There are now shushing phone apps for

parents, and a whole technique has grown around intermittent shushing and soft patting with the hand while rocking. It is called baby "white noise."

But David is doing the shushing here—he has learned to quiet his mind and turn his eyes from lofty visions to just be still and experience God. By simply taking time to do nothing but rest in God's presence, David finds his soul quieted. In Zephaniah 3:17 God is pictured as singing over us and quieting us with his loving presence. The repetition of the phrase "like a weaned child" in this psalm has the same calming effect and acts like a shush for our soul.

- What ways do you experience down time (such as David evidences in this psalm) in your schedule? Or what ways would you like to?

- What do you do when you are slowed down and have to wait in traffic or at the store checkout? How could you experience these in the spirit of this psalm?

- Is there anything in this psalm that you want to resist? What invitations are there for you in it?

# 5

# WASTING TIME JUST BEING

*She broke the jar and poured the perfume on his head.*
*Some of those present were saying indignantly to one another,*
*"Why this waste of perfume?"*

MARK 14:3-4

*Prayer is wasting time with God.*

THOMAS MERTON

*I* am sitting in a writing hermitage, a small one-room log cabin in the middle of a forest with windows on all sides, a small screened-in porch, a fridge, a microwave and coffee maker, a bed, an easy chair and a writing desk. It's the spring greening of the thousand-acre Clearwater Forest in northern Minnesota. I am here for a week, hoping to write every day. But I find that I need to just do nothing, fighting back feelings that I am off-plan, off-task and wasting time. I know better and should have planned on needing this down time to detach. But what has impressed me once again is how doing nothing, just being present to the woods and reading the book of God's creation, has restored me and my writing.

I am alone, but not alone, having met the same four deer three times a day on walks or when they pass by my window. The surprise we both feel when suddenly meeting each other on a path reminds me of the disciples' surprise when Jesus appeared after Easter. I stand transfixed by the blaze of their white tails amidst a verdant forest. The regreening of the brown decay makes me realize I am drinking in God's Easter-time re-clothing of the earth, his re-creating me and everything in his renewing love. Just as God renews his creation, God has re-created inner soul space for meeting him and others in my going to this holy place, this sacred space and time, to find him.

My image of Jesus has changed since seeing Luke's portrayal of him taking time away from ministry to enter into extended times of solitude. And my experience in the woods has me wondering what Jesus did during those times. Now that I have seen that he was not at the mercy of the crowd's demands and often left them for his own and his disciples' soul care, I no longer buy the Jesus-as-CEO approach, at least not the "driven for results" kind so often touted in books on how to lead like Jesus. Were Jesus' times away taken up mainly with planning sessions for his next ministry initiative or preparation of teachings and sermons?

My answer has come from examining his teaching. He does not give carefully constructed sermons exegeting Hebrew passages with well-reasoned outlines and points. He would not pass most seminary preaching classes. His teaching is mostly stories, parables and meditative observations of life, of both nature and people. The three-point sermons and lessons extracting propositional truths and how-to applications that we make out of these seem to miss the point; the medium, life itself, was his message. His preparation probably looked a lot like doing nothing other than being present to what was going on around him and noticing how God's rule, his kingdom, was manifested and how to join it. His times of solitude may have looked more like my first few days at the writing cabin than the last ones of furious writing.

Ann Rice, the famed vampire series writer, wonders about Jesus' formation and ministry too in her series on the life of Jesus. Along with the writings of N. T. Wright and his arguments for the resurrection of Jesus, she was moved by contemplating the beauty of cathedrals she was researching for her dark series. And she returned to her Roman Catholic faith, which is recounted in *Called Out of Darkness*. Rice wonders how the aesthetics of nature's cathedral formed Jesus.

As part of her current spiritual journey, she has removed herself from institutionalized Christianity, disappointed in much of its condemning and angry public face, to simply follow Jesus, a move that some think takes her farther away from Jesus. But I wonder if it isn't taking her closer. Rice remains in community with Christian friends and explains that her decision came as a result of her increased commitment to Christ, not less of one, a stand she felt she needed to make to stay true in following him.

In her *Christ the Lord* series of novels, *Out of Egypt* and *The Road to Cana*, she uses the apocryphal accounts of Jesus' raising fallen birds back to life as he learns how to work with his Father in heaven to do works of life-giving kingdom power. She imagines Jesus' prayer life and devotional practice, his familiarity with the psalter and Torah teaching. He has habits of being alone with his Father in favorite secluded spots near Nazareth. She depicts Jesus frequently contemplating both the psalms and what he observes in the created order, the stars at night, birds and trees, people in everyday life.

What did Jesus' rhythms of being with the Father look like? How might they relate to our own and to our life situation? As I have meditated on the sayings of Jesus in the Sermon on the Mount and other teachings, I believe that Jesus' advice to "consider the flowers of the field" and "the birds of the air" was a result of his own practice of doing nothing but taking in the chirping menagerie of a grassy meadow, a practice of Gregory of Nyssa, Francis of Assisi and Jonathan Edwards as well. As a child Edwards studied the "flying spiders" of the woods and noted the beauty of radiant rainbows. These musings were important to his sermons, particularly those on the divine light that warms both physically and spiritually.

At a two-week retreat where we were encouraged to take some time to "just do nothing," one participant decided to take a long walk without any particular purpose but to be present to creation. After a while he noticed he was becoming more aware of what was around him, taking time to stop to observe a rock or a plant or a tree. There were whole worlds in front of him that usually escaped his notice.

As he went along he came upon something he didn't quite know what to make of. What looked like a small lizard, about the size of one of his fingers, was wriggling on the ground, but something wasn't quite right with his head. As he stooped down to look at it, he realized that the lizard's head was stuck in an acorn shell. The lizard would struggle and then try to go on its way. Then it would struggle some more.

*What a strange sight*, he thought to himself. After spending time wondering how this lizard got into this predicament, he began to feel like he should help the lizard. So he gently took hold of the lizard's body and carefully removed the unwanted acorn cap. He placed the lizard on the ground and it stayed there for a little bit and then scurried off. As he continued to walk he often came back to the lizard and its acorn cap. It had to be symbolic. Something about the lizard's predicament began to touch him inside.

As he reflected on the week of retreat, a theme struck him, and the lizard put it all into perspective. He too was struggling with a kind of acorn cap, his head full of busy thoughts and plans, his life a constant rush of activity that kept him anxious and on the run. The retreat had slowed him down, particularly the requirements to sleep as long as he could and notice what his body was telling him, and to be okay with wasting time doing nothing. He had not been getting sleep like he was beginning to experience here. And the Scripture memorization had also worked to slow him down.

The walk, doing nothing, had been like a breath of fresh air to his soul, but the greatest present of all was the lizard. He had taken a picture of it just before setting it free of its burdensome cap. At the next day's session when it was his turn to share what God had been doing in his life at the retreat, he shared his lizard lesson. His only concern now was developing new habits in his life so that he didn't find his head stuck. How could he develop ways of restoring his soul, ways of regularly doing nothing, as part of his own soul care?

If we will not take time to shut down every once in a while and let our bodies, minds and souls just be, our bodies will rebel and shut down another way. There are records of leaders caught up in the unrelenting stress of their plans and conquests being suddenly struck by days of unexplained stupor. Their subordinates become unglued by the sudden change from brilliant and steady-as-a-rock leadership to a fearful puddle of tears or a dazed and confused stare. But King David's example in Psalm 131 shows us that we don't have to wait until we "tilt" to begin to practice downtime and the restorative power of doing nothing. We can learn to practice doing nothing regularly.

My own practice has been to let my golden retriever, Goldie, our black lab, Lady, or our cats be my guides for an afternoon. Watching them for a couple hours fight over a rope toy or retrieve a ball qualifies as wasting time for me. I also find just how much I am in my head when I waste time playing golf. This is done by going alone, by not keeping score or being my own constant critic and coach after each shot. I can't even keep a score card with me to find the next tee box or hole. I started out one time with a sense of freedom and relaxation, totally enjoying the release of hitting the ball and not really caring how I did. As you can guess, I started to play well and started to keep score.

Of course, golf is all about being relaxed and easy. The irony of playing well when I wasn't trying so hard has been a help in many things. Listening to people requires the same relaxed attention, not trying to find an answer to their problem or the right words in response. Being present to someone frees me up to give what is most needful.

It has also been great for my speaking. I can overprepare and still be working my outline in my head while I am presenting. Instead, I need to relax in my talk and be present to what I am saying and how people are receiving it.

Playing golf as a waste of time can sometimes be a wakeup call. One time I had taken the score card only to find that, halfway through only nine holes, I had lost my restfulness and started scribbling ideas down for the next week's talks. Since then, I have learned that I can trust God to bring ideas back to me when I am trying to do nothing.

## SABBATH AS A WAY OF BEING

In my last church I was given the gift of a sabbatical. Most sabbaticals are given as a desperate attempt to save a burned-out leader from quitting work altogether. Our leaders knew I was tired from a few years given to a building program and then a reorganization of staff, but they wanted me to take a sabbatical before I was desperate for one. The goals of the three-month sabbatical were for me to spend time with God and my family—just being with them. They did not require me to develop a study program or take training in some new skill. Being present to God and my family was to be my work. I studied how to make sabbaticals most effective and had a plan for intensive work with a spiritual director during the first two weeks of disengagement from work life and the last two weeks as I was preparing to reenter work.

That first week I began to slow down and had purposely not scheduled anything except the time with my spiritual director. I went to a coffee shop on the first day and noticed how fast I was walking—I had no appointment to get to, but my feet were going a hundred miles an hour. I had wanted this sabbatical to have a long-term effect on how I lived, and not just be a flash in the pan or little taste of slowing down that quickly faded. With that in mind, my speed walking into the coffee shop that morning got my attention.

So I decided right there, starting with my feet, to slow down. I actually stood in the parking lot for a moment and asked God to slow down my life, starting with my feet and my steps. And in a strange and backward imitation of routines I had developed in practice for sports, I counted out a very slow and steady pace for my walking rhythm, going slower as I went along and checking the automatic tendency to go faster. In the coffee shop I pulled out a book for a leisurely read and noticed how often I jerked my wrist up to check the time— but I had nothing to do for the whole day other than go to my late-afternoon appointment with my director.

About an hour into this luxurious first sabbatical day, with all going as planned, I got a call from my wife. "Hi honey! How is your *vacation* going so far today? Since you have nothing to do today, will you please go get some chemicals for my garden?" They could only be found at a store a couple hours away in Blaine, another suburb. "Vacation?" I responded with a bit of irritation in my voice, "I am on *sabbatical*, not vacation . . . and . . ." Just then the slowness that I had prayed for in my feet began to work in my tongue, and before I said what I was thinking, reminding my wife how I was doing nothing, which included chores for her, I found myself agreeing to get her chemicals—which would occupy the rest of my day, barely allowing for my trip to my director.

In the few seconds of our interchange God had reminded me of my sabbatical priorities—being present to God, my wife and kids. God made it clear to me that this particular errand may not be my definition of what was being present to my wife, but it was to God, and I was sure it would be to my wife too. So I put the book away for the next day and headed out for an afternoon of driving. It was another gift he gave me that day besides slowing down my steps in the parking lot. And God met me in that drive in a way that I doubt the book would have. In my great plans for my first sabbatical day I had in mind a great book to read. God had in mind doing nothing but driving with my mind on him on an ordinary chemical run to the other side of town.

My practice of doing nothing, of wasting time with God, often serves to help me be more aware of how driven I am by the tyranny of my agendas. Days of doing nothing are restorative in that we lay down our agendas, our self-important projects, and in the loss of our will we become more ready to do his will, and often that is serving him in a very ordinary thing done for another.

Please understand, I believe Jesus had very busy and full days, just as we often do. But besides working hard and long hours for days on end, I think Jesus had a practice of doing nothing as well. The one who took time to watch birds and flowers also took time to watch ordinary life and the people who inhabited it. His parables are largely the result, in my opinion, of great quantities of time doing nothing but being with God's creation. He had a rhythm of doing nothing often and long enough that he was available to do great things according to the Father's agenda, noticing and loving those who happened to be around him.

# Finding Our Rhythm
## *Taking a Day to Do Nothing*

Mark out a day when you and those in your group—whether individually, as a whole group, or in twos or threes—do nothing for an entire day. And if you practice this together, be careful not to make it a time of productivity. Just be together doing nothing. You aren't looking for any product or result but to be before God. One of my favorite ways to do this is to sit by the river and simply watch the flow of the water and observe the animals that come and go. I don't bring a camera or a notebook for a project. I do what I believe Jesus often did—nothing but observe the reality of life around him. He didn't do this to get a sermon or some illustration. It was to simply immerse himself in the reality of God's world.

Here are some suggested ways to do nothing. What would you add to the list?

1. Golf. Don't keep score or worry about how you are doing. Just play for fun and to be outdoors. Doing nothing while playing golf means not trying to improve your game or beat your best score or another person's. This might be tough at first, but notice why it is tough and let go of whatever gets in the way of just the delight of the sport.

2. Take a long leisurely walk along a lake or in a forest and

observe what goes on around you. The purpose isn't to write a piece about it or to produce any other product but to be in that space with God or another. Do not take a notebook, Bible or book—just spend time taking in creation and notice deeply what is in front of you, stopping at times to look intently at your surroundings and all it has for you to experience: sights, smells, sounds and textures. Use the eyes and ears of your heart.

3. Sit in a park or a public square and observe people. Watch their faces, their motion and activities. Make no judgment or attempt to understand or figure them out. Just be there.

4. Take a young child (or children), preferably around five and six years old, to a zoo, a museum or on a walk in nature—just follow their lead for at least a half day. You may need to give the child some options, but as much as possible let him or her dictate what you do and try to experience the day through the child's curiosity, inclinations and meanderings. Do whatever he or she wants to do. Don't lead; be led by the child. See the world through a child's eyes. Go without an agenda, letting your child guide you into his or her experience.

Reflect on your experience and share that with the group.

## Sounds of Silence: Psalm 65

Silence is praise to you,
   Zion-dwelling God,
And also obedience.
   You hear the prayer in it all.

We all arrive at your doorstep sooner
   or later, loaded with guilt,
Our sins too much for us—
   but you get rid of them once and for all.
Blessed are the chosen! Blessed the guest
   at home in your place!
We expect our fill of good things
   in your house, your heavenly manse.
All your salvation wonders
   are on display in your trophy room.
Earth-Tamer, Ocean-Pourer,
   Mountain-Maker, Hill-Dresser,
Muzzler of sea storm and wave crash,
   of mobs in noisy riot—
Far and wide they'll come to a stop,
   they'll stare in awe, in wonder.
Dawn and dusk take turns
   calling, "Come and worship."

Oh, visit the earth,
   ask her to join the dance!
Deck her out in spring showers,
   fill the God-River with living water.
Paint the wheat fields golden.
   Creation was made for this!
Drench the plowed fields,

soak the dirt clods
With rainfall as harrow and rake
    bring her to blossom and fruit.
Snow-crown the peaks with splendor,
    scatter rose petals down your paths,
All through the wild meadows, rose petals.
    Set the hills to dancing,
Dress the canyon walls with live sheep,
    a drape of flax across the valleys.
Let them shout, and shout, and shout!
    Oh, oh, let them sing! *(The Message)*

MOST TRANSLATIONS OR PARAPHRASES of this psalm render the first verse as "Praise awaits you, our God, in Zion." Although there is debate and translation of this passage is difficult, it is my belief that choosing the word *silence* is correct, especially when the context of the entire psalm is considered. As I have prayed the psalm, it invites me into the sacred space that silence creates. I think those who translate or paraphrase this verse as "silence is praise" are doing so from their formation in silence and wonder. Other translators may have no experience with silence; it is merely "dead air" to them.

Use your imagination as you enter into this psalm's two spaces, the temple and creation. First, we are quietly standing in the silent temple, God's house built with human hands (vv. 1-4). Then we are taken to all of creation, a house God built (vv. 5-13). In these two places, we also experience two kinds of silence. In the temple there is hardly any sound—it is a place for quiet gazing on God. Nature provides a different kind of quiet, the absence of words and talking.

In the temple we see one worshiping silently, having fulfilled a vow in the unspoken prayer of action and obedience rather than mere lip service. Next, we see a penitent person in tears over God's renewed forgiveness in response to a heart cry and hushed sobs for mercy. Then we are transported to a beach, a mountaintop or a wheat field. We hear the sounds of the earth and sky in the wind, rain, bird song, waves and streams, all in a dance that hushes the noise of the driven world.

- Imagine your favorite house of worship or sacred building where you have met God often in silence, whether alone or in a group. What is it like to be there? What feelings stir inside you?

- Imagine your favorite spot in creation—a beach, a mountaintop or a forest, a farmer's field or a meadow. What sounds do you hear, and what feelings do they evoke in you?

- Imagine being in the presence of a penitent person or a time and space in your life when great repentance and release were yours to give or receive. What feelings does that memory stir in you?

- Imagine being in the presence of someone you admire and respect, whose life speaks to you more than their words. What feelings does that memory stir in you?

- What roaring voices in our culture are in your ears constantly: Madison Avenue, politicians, the Dow Jones, Hollywood, the Internet? What are they telling you?

- How could our silence be considered praise before God?

## 6

# ENTERING INTO QUIET

*Be still and know that I am God.*

PSALM 46:10

*Silence is God's first language.*

JOHN OF THE CROSS

*I*t takes fourteen hours to fly from San Francisco to Tokyo, and maybe a few years or even a lifetime to get used to the cultural differences. It is a trip I have taken a number of times to teach and preach. On one trip I was able to go with my wife, Cheri, and experience Eastern culture and its unique mix of technological advances and ancient practices.

Cheri was amazed at the appliances that don't come to the United States, such as toilets with a control panel for warming the seat, playing music, dispensing deodorizer and personal hygiene. The top of the line is in the Guinness Book of World Records: Toto Company's Washlet, which has more than seven functions and thirty buttons on the control panel. And as of 2002 more than half the Japanese homes had a high-tech toilet, more than those with personal computers!

What is going on here is more than the Japanese knack for taking a

Western product and making it better. The Japanese take their individual and corporate peace of mind and body very seriously. But the biggest surprise occurred as we landed. After deplaning, we stood with hundreds of people from various flights to wait for our luggage. Cheri turned to me after a few minutes and whispered, "Something is wrong. Why is everyone so quiet?" She was experiencing a culture that is used to being quiet.

Japan knows something about silence. On the bullet train from Tokyo to Hiroshima, I was following my host through the various train cars, trying to carry on a conversation with him. Suddenly he turned around and without a sound put his finger to his pursed lips to quiet me. We were in what is known as a quiet car, not for sleeping necessarily, but for silence.

American culture does not value silence. It seems that we have to have a soundtrack going on wherever we are. From elevators to waiting rooms to radio chatter to iPods, we fill the air with sound. Gerald May, in his book *Addiction and Grace*, claims that the average American is so addicted to stress and noise that we cannot tolerate more than five minutes of silence. And for many Protestants the practice of silence is taboo and mistrusted; it is viewed as the province of New Age beliefs and liberal or mainline contemplative rituals.

But John of the Cross called silence "God's first language." God does not chatter at us most of the time. In fact, for most of our life he is quietly there with us, day and night. God does not advertise his presence. His works—trees and clouds—speak of him indirectly. His signature is subtly hidden on each one.

He hides most of the time. God is shy and does not usually press himself or his words on us, but wants dialogue. He speaks first by placing his Spirit in creation as his presence for us to pursue if we want. For those who are quiet, creation does speak, as Psalm 19 reminds us. His word through prophets and apostles speaks to us as well, but only as we are quiet enough for the Spirit to give us discernment.

Along with the rhythms of day and night and the seasons, God has wired his world and our bodies for rest and quiet. We require down time and sleep. So silence is not the invention of some religious guru or tradition, it is part of who God is, what he has made and how it functions best.

Even our listening to God should result in what Paul calls a quiet life: "Make it your ambition *to lead a quiet life*, to mind your own business and to work with your hands, just as we told you, so that your daily life may win the respect of outsiders and so that you will not be dependent on anybody" (1 Thessalonians 4:11-12). Paul was concerned that a noisy counterfeit of true spiritual life, self-centered and consisting of words only, would become a substitute for hands and feet that spoke of God's work.

This is the effect of Christian witness and work in the world, a quiet world where our words of prayer work for all of us that "we may live *peaceful and quiet lives*" (1 Timothy 2:2). Christian life is a hushing witness that tames and saves the roaring sea of humanity through the gospel for living in the truth. Paul undoubtedly got this from the prophets, such as Isaiah, who says that individual and national salvation come from being quiet enough to hear a whispering voice telling us which way to turn in life (Isaiah 30:15, 21).

Jeremiah writes that it is good for our spiritual growth that in our youth we *"wait quietly"* and "sit alone in silence" (Lamentations 3:26, 28). In Zephaniah God is like a mother who sings lullabies to express her delight and joy in a child. "The LORD your God is with you, . . . he will rejoice over you with singing" and will *"quiet you* with his love" (Zephaniah 3:17). Habakkuk proclaims, "The LORD is in his holy temple; let all the earth *be silent* before him" (Habakkuk 2:20), not referring primarily to the temple in Jerusalem, which was soon to be destroyed, but to the secure reality of his heavenly rule over all creation, a call that is echoed in John's description of heaven: "There was *silence* in heaven for about half an hour" (Revelation 8:1).

The climax of the singing voices of a multitude martyred but now worshiping with angelic hosts at God's throne in heaven is not a great crescendo but rather a half hour of silence. Imagine millions from every nation being silent and still before God, where it is so quiet for a half hour you could hear a pin drop. The psalms invite us to experience this kind of heavenly quiet and call us to "Be still and know that I am God" (Psalm 46:10; see also Psalm 37:7).

Observing how uncomfortable I can be when asked to be in quiet in worship services for even a minute, I wonder how we are going to be able to participate in that half hour before the throne. I have come to believe that quiet is a kind of nakedness of soul before God and each other. It removes our distracting talk, making us totally present to ourselves, others and God. Silence is how we get honest before God, without any words to dress up our reality.

What was Jesus' experience of silence? Did he teach on it? There are a few times we observe Jesus in silence or without words. When he is arrested in the garden and sent from Pilate to Herod, Herod questioned him at some length (Luke 23:8-12). And the chief priests and scribes were there, vigorously pressing their accusations. Pilate exclaims, "Do you refuse to speak to me?" (John 19:10). The text says that Jesus did not reply (John 19:9), neither answering the questions nor countering the accusations. He was silent. Isaiah 53:7 describes the suffering servant:

> He was oppressed and afflicted,
>> yet he did not open his mouth;
> he was led like a lamb led to the slaughter,
>> and as a sheep before her shearers is silent,
>> so he did not open his mouth.

Before being taken to Pilate and Herod, Jesus had been questioned by the chief priests and scribes. His words were few. His only answer had been to explain why he wasn't going to answer them, and a statement to the effect that he was placing his case and his life into God's hands, which they twisted to mean he was blaspheming and worthy of death.

The religious and political authorities were hoping to use Jesus' words to control and manipulate reality for their desired outcomes, silencing Jesus for good. I believe that Jesus' power over his own words in these most stressful and life-threatening situations, and his ability to quietly trust God rather than manipulate others with words, was due to his own practice of solitude and silence, in which he laid his soul naked before God. His advice about avoiding "many words" in prayer encourages this kind of silent baring of the soul to God. And in his admonition to not use lots of words in oaths, to give a simple yes or no, he extended this same naked transparency to others.

He practiced this same silence at the trial of the woman caught in adultery (John 8:4-11). The raging accusers kept asking him, "What do you have to say about this?" frustrated with his silent writing in the sand. And Jesus silenced them with a simple statement of his own, just a few words that revealed the falseness of their words and actions. "If any one of you is without sin, let him be the first to throw a stone at her." And then with a few words of forgiveness and challenge, he set the woman free. Jesus' practice of silence, not filling the air to paint false realities for himself or others, gave power to the words he did use.

At a retreat where we experienced twenty-four hours of silence, starting with our lunch and ending at lunch the next day, we felt awkward at first, using hand motions to pass the salt or water pitcher, but soon the silence opened up our sense of each other, so that we were aware of one another in a way our distracted talking could never provide. A kind of embarrassment, something like being naked in this silent lunch (although we were all fully clothed) was palpable, and I was eager to find out if others felt it too. We all did. And we surmised that it was due to the "clothes" of our words that kept our minds from a more direct and intimate experience of each other.

## CENTERING PRAYER

When I share the previous Scriptures with those I lead on retreats, they are quite amazed at how ignorant they are of silence in the Scriptures and how much our American culture has blinded us to the importance of silence. Traditions like the Quakers have nurtured and kept alive the corporate discipline of silence, so that it has become a part of how they do life together. Silence, for them, is an individual and a group activity, and it includes everything from worship to decision making to saying grace at meals. Lengthy pauses before answering questions or before praying to gather one's spirit up into God are common experiences. And even prayer is more often listening or just waiting on God, more the absence of words than speaking.

When a Quaker boy was allowed to sleep over at a friend's house, the hosts and parents, Christians themselves, asked if their young guest would like to say grace for the meal. He nodded his head yes, and all at the table, with heads bowed, waited for the boy to start praying. Several seconds went by. After a few more seconds, his embarrassed friend whispered to his mom, "He doesn't know how to pray; let me do it for him." The family knew nothing of holding silence together as a form of prayer. Their guest was already praying and was probably surprised they weren't as well. He just wasn't using spoken words.

In my former church we practiced centering prayer. It consists of finding a quiet place where we won't be interrupted and assuming a relaxed position. After a simple opening prayer we commit the time to God and place ourself consciously in God's presence. Then we grow quiet, letting our thoughts die down to nothing by the use of a prayer word to detach from our thoughts that inevitably come. At first, most who start to practice centering prayer find they are enslaved to their thoughts and easily distracted. But as they grow in the ability to be present to God, not seeking anything from him but his company, there is a deep peace that invades their being, the very peace of God's being.

Centering prayer (the prayer of quiet or prayer of the heart) is not about saying or thinking words, seeing images in our mind, or looking for an emotion. It is best described by the kind of down time we experience after talking with our best friend or spouse and there are no more words to say, no thoughts to herd into conversation and no feelings to express or entertain. We just enjoy being there with someone else.

One of the pastors I supervised came to me excited to share how centering prayer was working in her life. It was a practice we had learned at our annual staff retreat and incorporated into our ministry work together. And I had helped her in a recent physical ordeal she had undergone that week. She was the children's pastor, a small, petite woman full of energy. Although she had wrestled all her life with some physical diminishment due to a childhood disease, she didn't let it stop her from doing what she wanted to physically. So when she told me that she had dislocated her shoulder that week I didn't find it hard to believe.

What was more amazing was her story of how she helped the doctor with resetting her arm back into her shoulder, which is usually a very painful process. In order to correctly reset the arm and not bring more damage, the patient needs to fully cooperate, so he or she can't be put under anesthesia. So when my friend offered to help the doctor by practicing a form of relaxing prayer where the mind and the body lets go of trying to do anything, the doctor was intrigued and delighted to have this kind of patient.

My friend asked to have some time to center herself, briefly praying for God's gracious enabling and healing presence, not relying on technique or some self-effort but calling on God to act. She then did her part and started to relax on the table by slowing her breathing and not letting all the anxious thoughts, feelings and distractions change her focus. If she was distracted by something, she had a prayer word or phrase, such as the name of Jesus or the word *peace* to bring her back from the worrisome thought or feeling. She didn't worry about chasing these away (that would give them more power over her); she just let them go.

She had done this enough that she knew when she was centered or not; the inner calm and control to stay that way was now a habit and a familiar place in her body, mind, heart and soul. Doing this, she became like putty in the doctor's hands and arms, with a full will and consciousness to work along with the doctor's movement and direction. Soon her arm was fully in place and functioning like it always had.

Quietness and trust in God is what all our disciplines eventually should produce in us. It is a cultivated receptiveness to God that allows him to move in our hearts, our minds and even our bodies to cooperate with his leading and work for the kingdom. This kind of disengagement goes against so much in our culture. Therefore it is probably the most difficult for us to practice. But when we have done the hard work of being quiet long enough, the retreat center we build in our bodies allows us to be a calm and quiet refuge for others, a place where they can meet God and be quieted too.

# Finding Our Rhythm
## Watching *Into Great Silence*

Rent the film *Into Great Silence* through Netflix or purchase it at Amazon. It is about a worldwide religious order, the Carthusians, started about a thousand years ago by Brother Bruno, who wanted to live a life of silence. It is the strictest religious order when it comes to silence. The film's producer asked to make a film about the Carthusians' famous monastery in the Swiss Alps. He waited patiently knowing that time was different in this place of quiet.

Sixteen years later he got an answer. He could film under certain conditions so as not to disturb the community, which meant he would need to be with the monastery for the better part of a year to do so. The film's story is about the rhythms of the monastic life and includes the initiation and vows of a novice; individual and corporate prayers and liturgical worship; meals, work and play; the weekly brief time of conversation the monks are allowed; and a portrait of each monk silently staring into the camera.

The highlight is an interview with an elderly blind monk who shares his thoughts on God's love, life and death, the peace and joy he has found, and why he loves life so much at the monastery. His gentle and certain grasp of God's love is the fruit of learning God's first language, silence.

After viewing the film, reflect together on the following

questions. If possible, spend the day away, viewing this film with your group in total silence. Have a meal together before and after viewing the film, deciding ahead of time who will make each one so he or she can be quiet while preparing for everyone to eat. Set some time aside soon after the viewing to reflect on this experience and write what it meant to you.

1. What parts of the film were most engaging for you? What parts weren't?

2. What questions do you have about life in such a place? List these and try to answer them for each other from what you saw in the film.

3. What attracts you to this kind of life? Why?

4. What repels you from this kind of life? Why?

5. How did you experience each other at meals or during the day of silence? Were you more aware of each other's presence? In what ways?

# *Part Two*

# THE DANCE
# OF ENGAGEMENT

*I*n part two we will *engage* our ordinary relationships as well as our regular routines and schedules as places to find eternity breaking in. And in going along with Jesus and his disciples to be with the poor and marginalized, we will find the richness of our mutual dependency on God. In practicing examination and making amends, we will find the freedom of forgiveness and God's power for character that is perfected even in weakness. Finally, in viewing our life from the finish line of our death, life becomes a pilgrimage with others toward our home in God.

# Life Together: Psalm 133

How good and pleasant it is
    when brothers live together in unity!
It is like precious oil poured on the head,
    running down on the beard,
running down on Aaron's beard,
    down upon the collar of his robes.
It is as if the dew of Hermon
    were falling on Mount Zion.
For there the LORD bestows his blessing,
    even life forevermore.

THIS SHORT PSALM is in the collection of psalms called the Songs of Ascents, which were used as pilgrims made their way to the religious festivals in Jerusalem to celebrate with people from all over Israel. This psalm celebrates the unity of not only family and friends but also a whole nation and culture. It is ascribed to King David, who knew a deep and lasting friendship with Jonathan, the son of King Saul, who made David his rival and enemy. It uses a strange picture for friendship, portraying Aaron, Israel's high priest, being anointed with oil, with the oil dripping from his hair and beard, over his beautifully crafted robes.

This anointing ceremony was a symbol of the joy of deep relationships with God and others. Psalm 23 uses a similar image; enemies sit down for a meal and David's head is anointed with oil, symbolizing reconciliation and restored communion. Close friends sometimes rub each other the wrong way; sometimes that rub is very hard, like iron sharpening iron, as one proverb says (Proverbs 27:17). The psalmist recognizes this by saying how pleasant and good relationships can be, channels of experiencing God's blessing if they are in the context of God's transforming and redeeming power. The psalmist says these kinds of experiences are "precious," meaning that they can be rare. And when unity is disturbed, it is hurtful.

But the friendships that have overcome hurt and pain, and are oiled with God's forgiveness, grow even deeper and more blessed. Those kinds of relationships, whether in marriage, family or a group of friends, are the richest. Oil poured on a face makes it shine, and the beaming face of Israel's high priest was a picture of God's love reigning down on his people, making for harmony with each other and God.

As you read the psalm, picture those who are rich in relationship with you, those who make your face shine. These may be family, friends, coworkers or others.

- List three of your good friends (list more if you need to).

- Next to each name, put a few words that describe why each brings you so much joy.

- Take time to thank God for each by name, expressing why and how their relationship to you has blessed you, in both hard and good times.

- Write to or tell each person how they bless you and why. Make a note of their responses. What do you think blessed them in this act of appreciation?

# 7

# WRITING ON
# EACH OTHER'S HEARTS

*I no longer call you servants. . . . Instead, I have called you friends.*

JOHN 15:15

*Here we are, you and I, and I hope a third, Christ, in our midst.*

AELRED OF RIEVAULX

When I was in seminary I became good friends with David, an international student from West Africa. We grew close as we shared our calls from God, David to serve as pastor of his tribe, and my dreams for the same, a church somewhere in my country. David grew to trust me enough to show me pictures of his people and to share stories of how God had miraculously brought the gospel to them— stories he didn't share with Westerners due to his concern that they wouldn't believe him.

He asked me to not share these stories with others. I didn't then and still have held that confidence with him. David grew close enough to me that he began to share his irritation with Westerners' waste and lack of appreciation for simple things. I'll never forget the look in his eyes when he strongly but affectionately scolded me as we went to lunch. He has noticed how many towels I had pulled from the dispenser to dry my hands. "Did you really need all those?" he asked. I wasn't offended. I was actually quite honored to be rebuked by him—it showed how close we had become for him to be that honest with me.

He also was an encouragement to me in my faith journey. He would challenge me to give myself generously, what he called a one-hundred-percent commitment to God's work in me. And we prayed together. I will never forget his prayers. Their sincerity and power have contributed to my prayer life and hunger for God. Through David, God gave me a picture of my worldwide family in Christ.

I was also an encouragement to him, particularly in helping him understand cultural differences he was constantly running into. He felt safe enough to talk to me, asking questions and venting his frustrations.

Living in the school's dorm put David in many situations where he wasn't comfortable or was misunderstood. He had a habit of eating some very spicy food prepared with herbs that gave his dorm room and David himself a strong smell. One night during the dead cold of a Midwestern winter, all the dorm rooms suddenly heated up like ovens. When we complained, the resident assistant told us that the thermostat for the whole building was in David's room, so he asked me, David's friend, to see what was going on with the thermostat.

Oddly enough, David was not in his room and the RA decided to use his master key to get in. To our surprise, David was not only gone, but he had fully opened his window to the freezing cold air. With the window closed and the problem solved, we went to bed. Running into David the next day I asked him what had happened, why his window was open and where he had been that night. He told me with great shame that he had heard from another international friend that the dorm folks didn't like the smell of him or his room.

He was ashamed and decided to take care of it, leaving his room's window open to clear out the smell. I told him that no one meant him ill will, and we processed his embarrassment upon hearing how his solution to the problem had backfired.

Our friendship continued to grow in depth and intimacy, our differences not separating us but actually making us closer to each other—except for one week where I somehow offended David in a late night theological chat with a group of friends. We had been on opposite sides of a passionate debate that got a little heated. Eventually, as the evening went late, David ran out of steam and started to leave. As he walked out of my dorm room, I affectionately and a bit too loudly called out to him, "See you later, alligator!" hoping to leave the debate on a note of affirming our friendship.

An instant later David was back in my doorway, fuming. When I asked David why he was so upset, he changed his demeanor and calmly said, "Goodnight. It's okay." Then he turned and went to his room. Since it was so late, I decided to wait till the next day to ask him what it was all about. But he said he was being too sensitive and our friendship went on as good or better than ever.

A few years later, in sharing the incident with another person from the same country in Africa, I found out what had probably happened. With a laugh, my cultural interpreter explained that in that part of Africa, the very worst kind of verbal insult to give to your enemy was to call them an animal or give them an animal's name.

I laughed too at this cultural blunder of mine, and understood that as David stood in the hallway, he realized that I would never purposely insult him. He had given me the benefit of the doubt due to his trust in me.

Gratitude welled up in me for all the gifts that David and I had given each other during those two years. He had given me gifts of intimacy and vulnerability, understanding and mutual support, challenge and helpful debate, and forgiveness. Most of all, we had given each other our unfailing trust. I found in David the smell of a good friend, one that drips with the fragrant oil of a love that "covers over a multitude of sins" or that gives one another the benefit of the doubt.

We don't often see friendship, with all the ups and downs, as a discipline to cultivate. But it is where we learn to trust, forgive and be challenged for our good. A proverb says "faithful are the wounds of a friend" (Proverbs 27:6 ESV), which means a great blessing. Friends are like iron sharpening iron (Proverbs 27:17), even if there are a few sparks in the process. The best of friends have been sharpened, and trust between them is hard to break.

## JOURNALING ON THE HEARTS OF OTHERS

When Jesus tells his disciples that he no longer calls them servants but friends (John 15:15), we are hearing what they had come to mean to him—even in the face of his knowing they were about to forsake him. He demonstrates the great grace of giving them his forgiveness and trust, the greatest benefit of the doubt, as he tells Peter and the rest of them in that intimate upper room that he is going to lay down his life for them so they would have no doubt about his friendship.

My wife and I call each other best friends. My adult kids have also become my best friends. And it is in that formational space that we learn to daily lay down our lives for each other. As so often is the case in families, my daughter and I are in some ways more alike, and my son and my wife are alike in other ways. My daughter and I are more inclined to journaling and more easily spend time in solitude. My son and wife rarely journal, and although they practice solitude as a regular habit, they would rather write or journal in the space of relationships.

Many have written on the practice of having a soul friend and the sacred space that can be created between people who share deeply their spiritual journeys and experiences. But that kind of relational journaling isn't promoted the way that writing in a journal is. Jesus wasn't the only one who journaled on people's hearts. Paul also speaks of writing on hearts. He writes in 2 Corinthians 3:2-3, "You yourselves are our letter, written on our hearts, known and read by everybody. You show that you are a letter from Christ, the result of our ministry, written not with ink but with the Spirit of the living God, not on tablets of stone but on tablets of human hearts."

Surprisingly, science may back Paul's idea of correspondence in the hearts of those who are friends in Christ. The Institute of HeartMath has demonstrated that the heart has a kind of brain of its own, a separate nervous system responsible for the release of the chemical oxytocin, which in tests has been called the hormone responsible for our ability to bond with others and experience love.

This is good news for all of those who, like my wife and son, are not as drawn to journaling in books. And it should enlighten many of my students, most of whom are pastors and extroverts, who have gotten the impression that spiritual formation is only for the introverted, those who like to be alone and meditative rather than active and relational. It seems that this kind of journaling on hearts has been going on in the church for a long time.

## HOW JESUS INVESTED IN THE DISCIPLES' LIVES

While the Gospel of Matthew makes a quick transition from Jesus' temptation to his picking of the Twelve, in Mark and in Luke Jesus is pictured as spending a good deal of time with a larger group of disciples before he settles on calling the Twelve to a special ministry with him. In that time he visited their homes, families and towns, and observed them at their workplaces. John records that a few of the Twelve were with Jesus observing the ministry of John near Bethany outside of Jerusalem. It's possible they were there as part of pilgrimages to the feast celebrations that Jesus and his family customarily participated in.

So when Jesus prays all night and chooses the Twelve (Luke 6:12-16), he has already had some experience with these men. He had first called them to follow him as part of the larger group of apprentices that numbered at least seventy-two, those appointed to mission in Luke 10, and may have been as large as five hundred (1 Corinthians 15:6). It is interesting to note that the only description Luke gives in the list of the Twelve in Luke 6 is for Judas Iscariot, calling him the traitor. Having spent some time with them already, Jesus certainly could see the potential for good and bad in each.

Jesus makes himself vulnerable to these men. He even gets closer to three of them and picks one, John, to be his best friend. Jesus eventually transcended the master-apprentice relationship and called them his friends. As we look into Luke and the other Gospels to see the rhythms of Jesus' spiritual practices, spiritual friendship is probably one of the least imitated but is nonetheless presented as an example for us to follow.

In my ministry I remember an older pastor telling me to "never make or have close friends at your church." I have had enough bruises and betrayals from many church relationships to appreciate why he told me that. And in my pastor-to-pastors role, I have heard many more. But I have also had more than enough comfort and encouragement from a few close and faithful friends in ministry to put the bruises and betrayals in perspective.

Being protective and overly cautious in relationships is not how I see Jesus' humble and vulnerable example of leadership. I have made a study of Jesus' last few interactions with Judas, whose name is now a synonym for unfaithfulness. I used to interpret Jesus' words in reaction to Judas's kiss in the garden as an expression of his anger and contempt. He said, "Judas, are you betraying the Son of Man with a kiss?" (Luke 22:48), and "Friend, do what you came for" (Matthew 26:50). I have now come to see Jesus' every interaction with his apprenticed enemy, even that kiss, as acts of love, calling out to Judas that it is never too late to repent. He could have exposed Judas to the sword-wielding Peter before that last kiss. Even in that kiss, Jesus still calls him "friend."

More remarkably, on the night that he predicts his disciples will abandon him, he tells them they are no longer apprentice servants. They have become his beloved friends. In his great friendship, he looks beyond their abandonment and cares for their grief and confusion, praying for them, and asking his Father to protect them.

Jesus wants them to know that whenever two of them are together, they share in his befriending presence. It is remarkable that more isn't made of the spiritual discipline of friendship. Perhaps it is such an ordinary and basic part of life that we neglect to see its power and place in our lives. This was not true among the ancient masters of the spiritual life. Even friendships between men and women were cultivated.

## FRANCIS AND CLARE

St. Francis had a friend in the young woman Clare. She was cloistered and didn't travel as he did in his mendicant order. Francis referred to a cell of the heart, what we have called a retreat center in the heart. He told Clare that just as she was in her cell in the cloister, he was in the cell of his heart. And that she could develop a cell in her own heart. People could travel the world and own nothing yet have a home everywhere they went by entering the cell within their hearts.

If Clare could develop this cell in her heart, even though she wasn't on the road and didn't feel her life was as exciting as Francis's, she could find a lifetime of travel and adventure in her daily meetings of deep contemplative prayer with the Lord. He promised that the room within her heart would grow until Francis, all the brothers, all the Poor Ladies and the townspeople could fit into her cell. She would thrive from an inexhaustible well—the cell God made in her heart.

# Finding Our Rhythm
## *Taking an Intercessory Prayer Flight*

An often-overlooked discipline of friendship is intercessory prayer. I have a prayer routine for intercession that I developed over the years. On Monday I pray for my immediate family and all my relatives. On Tuesday I pray for all those over me in authority, at work, in the church, and local and national leaders. Wednesday and Thursday I pray for those I work with in my various responsibilities, students in my classes, readers of books, retreat participants, and those I coach and mentor. On Fridays I pray for my *friends,* my enemies and my mentors.

On Saturdays and Sundays I use a map of the world and one of the United States. Saturdays I pray for the whole world by continents, moving from my home to the east and back again. I pray for God's kingdom to come, and as the Spirit leads me I pray for particular countries that have been in the news and especially for "the least of these" in these countries. On Sunday I make the same route, but pray for the body of Christ on each continent, especially for those undergoing persecution and imprisonment. I have many friends in these places, and praying for them is a great way to keep in touch with them.

Develop a prayer flight as a group. Include prayer for your group members by assigning days when you will intercede

for each other so that the whole group is praying for the same person on the same day. Then have each person share what they would specifically like prayer for in the coming four weeks or until you meet again. Be detailed about what results you want them to pray for in your life.

Have each person share a world situation they are most interested in praying for, and decide together as a group which of these you can all pray for. Keep up with the news so you know what is happening there. Pray for the church in that area as well, and try to find out what needs the church might have in that area so you can pray specifically. As you pray for one another and the world keep these questions in mind and be ready to share your answers at the next group meeting.

- What was your experience of praying for the other members of the group? What results did the person see *in him- or herself* while praying for the others in the group? More compassion or interest in each person? Did you get any sense of what God is doing in the other person as you prayed? What results were there *in the situation* the person specifically asked you to prayer for?

- What was your experience of praying for a part of the world? Did you sense more of a solidarity with the people of that place?

## Night and Day Prayers: Psalms 4–5

Answer me when I call to you,
 O my righteous God.
Give me relief from my distress;
 be merciful to me and hear my prayer.

How long, O men, will you turn my glory into shame?
How long will you love delusions and seek false gods?

Know that the LORD has set apart the godly for himself;
 the LORD will hear when I call to him.

In your anger do not sin;
 when you are on your beds,
  search your hearts and be silent.

Offer right sacrifices
 and trust in the LORD.

Many are asking, "Who can show us any good?"
 Let the light of your face shine upon us, O LORD.
You have filled my heart with greater joy
 than when their grain and new wine abound.
I will lie down and sleep in peace,
 for you alone, O LORD,
  make me dwell in safety. (Psalm 4)

Give ear to my words, O LORD,
 consider my sighing.
Listen to my cry for help,
 my King and my God,
  for to you I pray.
In the morning, O LORD, you hear my voice;
 in the morning I lay my requests before you
  and wait in expectation.

You are not a God who takes pleasure in evil;
    with you the wicked cannot dwell.
The arrogant cannot stand in your presence;
    you hate all who do wrong.
You destroy those who tell lies;
    bloodthirsty and deceitful men
    the Lord abhors.

But I, by your great mercy,
    will come into your house;
in reverence will I bow down
    toward your holy temple.
Lead me, O Lord, in your righteousness
    because of my enemies—
    make straight your way before me.

Not a word from their mouth can be trusted;
    their heart is filled with destruction.
Their throat is an open grave;
    with their tongue they speak deceit.
Declare them guilty, O God!
    Let their intrigues be their downfall.
Banish them for their many sins,
    for they have rebelled against you.

But let all who take refuge in you be glad;
    let them ever sing for joy.
Spread your protection over them,
    that those who love your name may rejoice in you.
For surely, O Lord, you bless the righteous;
    you surround them with your favor as with a shield. (Psalm 5)

THESE ARE PAIRED PSALMS that play off each other. And they were used
in the liturgical life of Israel as evening and morning psalms. Psalm 4

encourages us to not let the night's dark cause us to stop looking into the light of God's presence and peace. Nighttime is often a time when our fears and insecurities take hold of us. As children, many of us were afraid of the dark and took comfort from a nightlight in the hall. The psalm encourages us to invite God into our night. It discourages fretful worry and anger that come when we are restless about some problem and are tempted to sin in our thoughts by relying on our own strength and wisdom instead of trusting God.

Psalm 5 in turn invites us to not begin our day alone and rushed but to bring our expectations for our day to God and keep going to him as a refuge when we encounter and are tempted by the evil of our fallen world. The writer bows down toward the temple and keeps that posture in his spirit, crying out for God's sheltering mercy throughout the day.

The rhythms of these psalms start with night in Psalm 4 and end with daytime. The Hebrew rhythm of night to day runs counter to how we usually mark our days. These psalms reflect the Hebrew idea of how to go to God over twenty-four hours. The day starts at night before we go to sleep, not when we get up in the morning. The sabbath reflects this: it starts on Friday evening and ends at dusk the next day. And the day ends with the cessation of your day's activities. The night is a restorative time that feeds our next day. The desert fathers thought that nighttime was when the devil is most active and therefore was a time to be extra vigilant. So they offered this time to God. Therefore Psalm 4, an evening psalm, is first, followed by Psalm 5, a morning psalm.

- Try using the Jewish rhythm of starting your cycle of prayer with an evening "quiet time" instead of a morning one. Read and pray Psalm 4 at night and Psalm 5 in the morning for the entire week. At the end of the week, record your reflections and share them with your group.

- Psalm 4—Evening reflections. First, what are you thankful for as you close this day with God (vv. 5-7)? How has he "shown the light of his face" to you? What put a smile on your face today? And what were the times today when you think God was "smiling down" on you and those you love? Second, what are the day's distresses and upsets that you need to bring to God and leave with him as you lie down and sleep (vv. 1-4, 8)?

- Psalm 5—Morning reflections: First, what expectations do you have for this day? Share them with God. What requests do you need to make of God this day (vv. 1-3)? What about this day do you need to trust to God's will and his timing for resolution (vv. 4-6, 9-10)? Second, what or who do you need to place in God's presence, for his leading and blessing today (vv. 11-12)?

# 8

# USING EARTHLY ATTACHMENTS
# FOR A FIX ON ETERNITY

*Each day Jesus was teaching in the temple,*
*and each evening he went out to spend the night*
*on the hill called the Mount of Olives.*

LUKE 21:37

*How can we pray to Him without being with Him?*
*How can we be with Him without thinking of Him often?*
*And how can we think of Him but by a holy habit we should form of it?*

BROTHER LAWRENCE

*D*amon asked me for prayer after I had preached the sermon "Slowing Down Enough to Go at God's Speed—The Speed of Love and Relationships." He definitely needed some slowing down. My experience with him would teach me that God can use our compulsions and addictions and the speed of their furious appetites to bring us to an end of ourselves and ultimately slow us down. But God also can use these cravings, when detached from these idols and attached to him, to bring us into a life that is more peaceful and centered on him and others rather than ourselves and our idols.

He was in the midst of a raging storm in his life, a storm of chasing dollars and the career ladder—which included the announcement that his wife and their little girl were moving out because of his anger, stressful lifestyle and emotional unavailability. He knew he needed to slow down and was hungry for the "peace and quiet" of a slower pace.

Contributing to his stress was his failure in the frenetically paced job he held in finding financing for initial public offerings on the stock market. His sales had trailed off to almost nothing and he was going down the tubes, fearing the loss of his employment. He was now desperate and suddenly alone. He wanted things back where they had been—and as soon as possible—with God's just-in-time inventory of quick help and my speedy intercession for it.

You've seen people like Damon pacing down airport terminals with their Bluetooth headsets, talking loudly to no one you can see. That picture had become his life. Talking unceasingly and making deals with no one he could see, he was missing his loved ones who were right in front of him. After praying for him, we agreed to meet for coffee the next day. We met downtown on his turf at a coffee shop. After filling me in on more of the details of the problems we had prayed for at church, he added, "And by the way, I also want to quit smoking too."

I had already been overwhelmed with his situation and now he wanted to do what most people can't do in the best of circumstances! He was going for the whole enchilada! He was going to reform himself all the way and get his life back where he wanted it! I felt like I was facing an impossible challenge. Without letting on that I was overwhelmed with his situation, and trying to find some way to genuinely help him, I kept asking questions, stalling for a flash of insight or comforting word that would connect him with God, while at the same time trying to figure out how to let him down easily from his expectations of a quick fix.

And then it came to me. God spoke as clear as a bell: "Tell him not to try to stop smoking. Tell him to use the cigarette as a way to remember to take the whole situation to me and leave it there." So I obeyed and found myself saying these unconventional words of pastoral advice: "Damon, why don't you go to God like you go to your cigarette?"

This advice came to me as a consequence of my own constant practicing the presence of God and shooting up one of those "Help me God, I don't know what to do" prayers. I had been obsessively trying to go to God throughout my day, trying to be open to his voice and receptive to his leading and direction. But "go to God like a cigarette" was not what I was expecting from God as an answer to this man's needs. I explained that God was good, really good, in fact better than we can imagine. God is more interested in Damon's trusting his goodness than concerned now with Damon's cigarette habit. Instead, he was more interested with Damon's beginning to trust him with the mess he made of his life.

Cigarettes were certainly bad for Damon, but not as bad right then as the way Damon was losing himself and his family in the pace and direction of his life. In fact, going to God as he went to his next cigarette was probably perfect timing, because the stress that caused him to reach for the next nicotine relief was what he needed to bring to God. And God was not so stingy with his mercy that he wouldn't wait with his help and grace until Damon stopped smoking. God would even use Damon's smoking to grace Damon into God's love and peace.

Damon said he'd try it for the next two weeks and let me know what happened when we next met. I didn't think he would do it—it was kind of strange advice from a pastor and was also a crazy obsessive solution to an already out-of-control habit. Two weeks later he couldn't wait to tell me what had happened. His wife and little girl were still gone and his job situation was still looking bleak, but to his surprise our little experiment in practicing God's presence with the help of several packs a day had resulted in some amazing peace for the first time in his life. There was this sense of quietness and well-being that was becoming a bottom line for him and allowed him to stop obsessing about his family and job. He was beginning to trust that God would take care of it.

And then with an awe that most reserve for describing a trip to the Rocky Mountains or the Grand Canyon, Damon said that as he sat in his office and smoked and prayed, he saw for the very first time that there was this beautiful tree outside his office window. As he took in the beauty of the tree, he saw a squirrel! It was amazing! All this was right outside his window all the time. For all the times he had sat there looking out that window he hadn't noticed the beautiful creation all around him.

We talked at length about how his slowing down had opened him up to a world bigger than the cramped world he had reduced his life to and had cut his family out of. He was seeing God and even God's creation. And maybe soon he could see his family back with him because he would be seeing them with the kind of attention and engagement he had reserved for making deals.

I wondered if he kept up turning to God in prayer whether the cigarette would eventually fall out of his hand because his hand would now be fully grasped in God's gracious grip. Damon's practice illustrates how we can take some of our attachments that need to be transformed and use them as prayer bells to take us into God's presence.

## UNDERSTANDING RHYTHMS

I have learned to look for places in my life where I can attach a spiritual practice in order to make that practice easier to incorporate into my life. This led to my practice of praying my day. Instead of relying on only random spontaneity in trying to connect with God during the day, I started uttering a short prayer to be open to God, asking him to be with me before or after meeting with someone. Or I would make the day's project or work items a place to invite God in.

God has built rhythms into creation and our very being. Our bodies are tuned to the rhythms of day and night, called circadian rhythms, as is much of animal and plant life. Then there are the tides that sway to the pull of the moon and seasonal cycles coming from earth's orbit. And every farmer knows that there is a need for his land to rest and be replenished, just as the winter gives the farmer that same time for rest. When God gave Moses the law, he instituted social rhythms of rest every week on the sabbath. Soldiers too were given a year to be with their newlyweds, and every seventy years the whole land was given a jubilee rest.

There is an irony that Jesus became human and submitted himself to rhythms he created. So when Jesus rebukes his critics for their disapproval of his doing good deeds of healing on the sabbath and declares that the sabbath is made for humans, not humans for the sabbath, he isn't merely correcting their theology and practice, he is speaking as an artist in disguise, one who knows how his creation is supposed to work.

We are told that it was Jesus' custom or habit to observe sabbaths and religious feasts, making the yearly pilgrimage to Jerusalem from Galilee. Jesus also used the rhythms of the temple. And his disciple's request that Jesus teach them how to pray shows that he had a prayer rhythm as well. And from Peter's example, we know Jesus' disciples prayed at fixed hours, as did all pious Jews (see Acts 10).

## PRAYER RHYTHMS

I have found that God respects our prayer routines and meets us there. Several times I have been given a sense of God's direction while I have been in prayer, both in my own fixed-hour prayer times and in those times of praying though my day. One time as I was interceding for a younger relative who was in some trouble with the law, I felt led by

God to drop my prayers and be with this young man. It was a critical time in his life, and he needed someone to help him weather the storm and submit himself to some corrective discipline.

Having regular rhythms of prayer is like having your cell phone turned on to be able to hear someone trying to get your attention. By having times in our day's routine to check in with God, we turn our attention "on" to God; without these rhythms, we are "off" on our own. We become receptive to God's voice and leading by practicing rhythms of prayer. This kind of fixed-hour prayer has been the practice of God's people from the time of Israel to today. At the time of the Reformation the abuses that had occurred during the medieval monastic period caused many to see fixed prayer and the use of prayer books as tainted and leading to works that attempted to earn God's favor.

Phyllis Tickle's *Divine Hours*, three books of weekly and daily fixed-hour prayers based on the Anglican Book of Common Prayer, has helped many with this ancient practice. Stopping and praying at fixed hours during the day places a person within a worldwide chorus of unceasing prayer. The prayers have times of special confession on Fridays. They also incorporate the church's calendar with special prayers and readings from Scripture for the three main seasons of Advent (from late November through to just after Christmas), Lent (from before Ash Wednesday to Easter) and Ordinary Time (after Easter until late November).

These aids help keep our lives in God's great drama of redemption and not just in the world's story of taxes, summer vacations, athletic seasons and paid holidays. For many Christians the only "seasons" they recognize are Christmas Day and Easter. And although we can make a deadening and legalistic ritual of observing religious days and seasons, when these rhythms are done in faith, by God's grace they can open our lives to something much greater than the stories of our sports teams or a nation's cultural celebrations.

## PSALMS AS ANTIDOTE

Just as Psalms 4–5 help me end and start my day, Psalms 130–131 help me turn to God during moments of the day. They have helped me with my greatest attachment, not to a job or some drug, but to my ego and its fallen habit of trying to live apart from God and his power. Echoing the hymn writer's cry, I am "prone to wander Lord, I feel it, prone to leave the God I love." Ken Blanchard, the management guru who found Christ, says that ego stands for "edging God out." The regular reciting and meditation on Psalms 130–131 help me turn to God when I find myself tempted to edge God out.

I find myself responding in one of two sinful ways to my life's circumstances, responses that have now become attached to my way of doing life. When I have failed or sinned, I find that instead of confessing my sin, which means agreeing with God about it and asking for his forgiveness, I try to take care of it on my own by shaming myself and dwelling on it. I am attached to habits of self-condemnation that lead me to negative self-talk and a spiral of "practicing the presence of my sin," ending up with a state of depression and isolation from God and others.

The other sinful response is occasioned by a success or something good I have done. Instead of being humbly thankful, I use it as an opportunity to indulge my fleshly need for empty, self-centered praise. I start a subtle, self-congratulating "practice of my own presence" that spirals up and up until the inevitable fall that always accompanies this kind of pride. Then I feel like a failure and start the downward spiral to depression.

This can become a life of cycling through ups and downs, living without Christ and on my own, not by his grace. The two psalms break this cycle. Psalm 130's opening cry, "Out of the depths, I cry to you, O LORD," and the reminder that God is not a God who counts sin against us takes me out of my negative spiral to a place of peaceful repentance and God's presence.

Psalm 131's opening declaration, "My heart is not proud, O LORD, my eyes are not haughty," and its picture of King David's stilling his soul of his grandiose plans, becoming like a weaned child with his mother, keeps me out of my puffed up self-praise. It helps me stay in dependent rest and have an appropriate appreciation of my part in things, guarding my heart against robbing God of his glory and gifts to me, with him, not me, being my ultimate good.

I have even adapted the use of these psalms in my golf game. Golf is a lot like life, with its ups and downs, the need to recover from errors and stay centered on the game and not self-performance. It is a good reflection of my life's need for constant repentance and dependence. So in order to keep these psalms on my mind and heart, I mark one golf ball with the number 130 and the two words *have mercy*, for when I am tempted to give up hoping to doing better. And I mark a ball with a 131 and the two words *not proud* when I am doing well and am tempted to become self-conscious of my good score and play. This helps me be attentive, staying focused on the next shot's opportunity and not the last one's glory or failure.

## THE POWER OF ROUTINES

In *The Power of Engagement*, Jim Loehr and Tony Schwartz explain the importance of rituals and routines that energize and keep focus in the lives of high-performing athletes, rituals that make use of ordinary life rhythms, both disciplines of engagement and disciplines of disengagement. Their book has simply taken what God has wired into humans and the Scriptures, and what the great masters of spiritual life have used to partner with God, and used them for their sporting successes.

Paul and biblical writers use these training metaphors. We can use our life's attachments, routines and rhythms to live fully engaged with God and others. Of course these rituals can lose their meaning, just as saying grace before a meal has for many who are not actively seeking to partner with God. Sometimes, to keep the focus, we need to renew the practice with slight changes. For a while, when our children were young, we kept our eyes open when praying table grace, not as a gimmick but as a way of becoming more present to God and each other. Closing eyes during prayer is intended to focus those praying on their prayers. Opening our eyes restored the same intended result. When the outward behavior of the ritual becomes the focus, we need to review our rituals.

The Pharisees were legalistic about washing dishes and lost the power of this practice illustrated in the Hebrew law books. In *Rules of Holy Living and Dying*, Jeremy Taylor, the seventeenth-century Anglican divine, advocates using ordinary routines to make us attentive to God, such as using our morning or evening washing to remind us to ask God's Spirit to wash our minds and bodies with renewing graces. At a Greek Orthodox friend's house, I noted the little hand-painted sign in the bathroom that read, "Lord, cleanse us from all sin, even as we cleanse our hands for your service."

The rhythms of life, such as daily meals, personal hygiene, getting up in the morning and going to sleep, are opportunities to fill our lives with God's presence and partnering. These are not the inventions of strange religious traditions but are the way God made us to function in life. The formal study of daily, tidal, weekly, seasonal and annual biological rhythms is called chronobiology and reflects a divine ritual built into life. God has created within us a human clock based on regular twenty-four-hour cycles. The following exercise employs the psalmist's practice of praying seven times a day, but it uses a New Testament prayer—the Lord's Prayer.

# Finding Our Rhythm
## *Praying Seven Lord's Prayers a Day*

Memorize your favorite version of the Lord's Prayer (Matthew 6:9-13 or Luke 11:2-4) or the following Dallas Willard paraphrase of the Lord's Prayer. Write it on a piece of paper to keep with you. Pray it when you first get up, before you eat breakfast, lunch and supper, and before you go to bed. Do this for a week (or even a month).

> Dear Father always near us,
> > May your name be treasured and loved.
> > May your rule be completed in us.
> > May your will be done here on earth
> > in just the way it is done in heaven.
> Give us today the things we need for today,
> > and forgive us our sins and impositions on you
> > as we are forgiving all who in any way offend us.
> Please don't put us through trials,
> > but deliver us from everything bad.
> Because you are the one in charge,
> > and you have all the power,
> > and the glory too is all yours—forever.
> Which is just the way we want it!

After a week (or month) of using this prayer, take a half day (with your group, if possible) to meditate on and pray

over the following questions. Discuss your experience with your group.

1. In the past week, what ways have you sensed God as your loving Father? What has your experience been of his presence on a daily and moment-by-moment basis?

2. Can you name an area of your life where, in the past week, you have come to more fully desire God's full reign and glory to be revealed?

3. In the past week, what needs have you seen God meet?

4. In the past week, what has your sense of God's forgiveness been? In your forgiving others?

5. In the past week, what bad experiences were you delivered from? How did that deliverance come about?

6. In the past week, where did you sense God's glory being displayed (his will clearly followed) or his power at work and his authority exercised in your life?

## A Clean Record: Psalm 130

Out of the depths, I cry to you, O LORD;
    O Lord, hear my voice.
Let your ears be attentive
    to my cry for mercy.

If you, O LORD, kept a record of sins,
    O Lord, who could stand?
But with you there is forgiveness;
    therefore you are feared.

I wait for the LORD, my soul waits,
    and in his word I put my hope.
My soul waits for the Lord
    more than watchmen wait for the morning,
    more than watchmen wait for the morning.

O Israel, put your hope in the LORD,
    for with the LORD is unfailing love
    and with him is full redemption.
He himself will redeem Israel
    from all their sins.

PSALM 130 IS ONE OF THE TWO psalms written about in the last chapter. Besides its help for me in ego attachments, it helps me get in touch with the areas of my life where I need forgiveness and hope to defeat and be delivered from sins I have a tendency to commit time and again. The psalmist starts out overwhelmed by the depth of his sin. He ends with the hope of the eventual deliverance from every sin in life.

This is one of five psalms called the penitential psalms. Each one involves some repentance and acknowledgement of sin, and the need for forgiveness and restoration with God and others. It uses the image of the night watchman who is waiting to be delivered from the darkness of night. The psalmist cries for mercy from the "depths" of his darkest sin, his brokenness.

At the same time he knows that God does not keep a record of sins and is unfailing in his love and forgiveness. But the psalmist doesn't just want a sin or some sins to be forgiven, he wants to be delivered from all sin. And he wants this for his community and nation as well. He is certain that God has promised to do so. So he waits for God's full deliverance. The psalm not only is a place to be reminded of forgiveness and deliverance but lays the basis for regular practice of examining our lives and making appropriate amends, which frees us to enjoy life to the fullest with each other.

- What do the depths of your sin look like? Which sins are deeply ingrained in you and require a deeper sense of God's unfailing love to deal with over a lifetime?

- What would your life be like, your experience of others, if these sins were less of a force in your life?

- How do you react when someone shines a light on some blind spot of yours? Are you getting more defensive or less so? How would your relationships change for the better if you became more grateful and willing to see yourself through their eyes? What if you were eager to further examine this area of your life with their help and encouragement?

# 9

## ASKING FORGIVENESS
## OF ANOTHER

*First go and be reconciled to your brother;*
*then come and offer your gift.*

MATTHEW 5:24

*The liberation experienced by the man*
*who has confessed his sins is . . . contagious.*

PAUL TOURNIER

*J*im told me the story of finding forgiveness for his sins in a relationship that had taken place many years earlier. It was a healing
experience.

In college he had dated a girl named Becky and eventually they
were engaged. But as they progressed in their commitment to each
other Tim found that his parents were beginning to disagree with the
couple's plans to simultaneously pursue graduate education after graduating from college. Becky had a few thousand dollars in school loans,
which seemed like a lot of debt to carry into marriage. There were
other problems for Tim's parents that became issues for Tim. For example, Becky's parents weren't as conservative in their lifestyle. Soon

Tim confronted Becky about her debt, her family history and other matters that hadn't mattered to him before his parents had pressed him about them.

Now looking back on that time, after doing some of the same work with his parents intruding in his current marriage, and with the clarity of some therapeutic space to revisit those memories, Tim found that the fight with Becky had been more about his parents than about him. And he was sorry about how he had treated her. These issues had disrupted their relationship and Tim, had broken up with Becky. Becky had thought they could work it out.

For the last fifteen years Tim was happily married to Mary. They had three children and a strong marriage and home life. But Tim's parents were once again intruding, and Tim and Mary sought counseling about it. So when he told Mary about his counseling discoveries about his past, his former engagement and his parent's interference, Mary understood how that felt and was remarkably mature about the whole matter. She agreed that for Tim's full healing of this wounded past and freedom for their present, he would need to pursue closure with Becky and his parents.

Becky was now married too and had a family. After looking up Becky's contact information and calling her, Tim explained the nature of his call, the program he was working on and that his wife, Mary, was in support of this work. He shared that he was in the process of listing those he felt he had hurt, and as part of his work he was making amends with those he could, at least saying he was sorry and owning his actions that hurt others. In this case, he said he wanted to talk about why they broke up, wondering if Becky knew why.

He made it clear that if this was not something she wanted to do or if she became uncomfortable at any time with the process during the call, he would understand, thank her for even considering it and do the work on his own. Becky was intrigued with the twelve-step work because her sister was part of the same program. She was okay with it.

She answered his question about her understanding of the breakup, explaining that she never really knew why.

Tim explained that he now realized that much of what had happened was due to his parents' problems with Becky's family and their general dislike of Becky, so he had acted more to please them than knowing his own mind on the relationship.

He further explained that in counseling he had been asked to go over his life in periods of ten years, and when he got to his twenties and started explaining the breakup shortly after the engagement, he started feeling very angry about it all. And as he told the story to his counselor, he could see what happened more clearly.

He knew his parents didn't intend to hurt anyone, and thought they were trying to give good parental advice, but they also had a pattern of pressing too hard for what they wanted for their kids, not respecting their adult children's need to decide for themselves.

Tim wrapped up his call with an apology for how they broke up, the confusion it created and the hurt that resulted. He acknowledged his fault in not realizing this at the time and for letting his parents influence him too much and not standing up to them. Becky thanked Tim for taking the time to call her about this and said she respected what Tim had done, which helped her understand things a little better.

## MAKING AMENDS

The eighth step of Alcoholics Anonymous involves making "a list of all persons we [have] harmed, and [becoming] willing to make amends to them all." And then the ninth step is the process of making "direct amends to such people wherever possible, except when to do so would injure them or others." Those who have followed these steps do an incredible amount of work with family, friends and anyone they have harmed, giving release not only to themselves but also to those ready for that kind of restoration. Step ten involves continuing "to take personal inventory and when we [are] wrong promptly [admitting] it," which just keeps the amends work up-to-date and results in a lifestyle of immediate restoration, living in reconciled relationships.

The key to this work is that it is done directly if possible, meaning a face-to-face encounter with the person if he or she is willing. If the person is not willing, the amends can be made to a substitute, a sponsor, pastor or other person who can give the gift of hearing the person's amends work and give him or her completion. Tim's amends would have needed to be done with someone other than Becky if she was not willing to participate.

The other key is that amends does not do further harm to the other person or persons involved in the amends process. This was where it was important for Tim to be sure that first of all his current relationship with Mary would not be harmed in any way by his work with Becky, and that Becky's relationship with her husband wasn't harmed.

This kind of work is foreign to most Christians today, but for most of the Christian tradition it wasn't. In the historic Eastern and Western churches, confessing small and large sins was an important step in living free from guilt and shame. It involved a careful time of review and examination of life and bringing any sins to God and a witness. At the very least it involved sharing how our sins have hurt others and having someone help us place our faith in God's forgiveness and freedom from these sins and their consequences. The idea of penance originally was much more like the ninth step—making amends, not earning anything from God.

In the film *The Mission* the main character is a violent mercenary and slave trader who harms South American indigenous people. He also kills his own brother who had fallen in love with his fiancé. He makes a confession of faith, showing remorse over his life and his treatment of people. So he takes a trip back to the places he has pillaged, hauling his armor and weaponry in a great sack on his back. At one point as he climbs a mountain path to his destination, the great weight causes him to stumble. A priest sees his burden, both on his back and in his heart, and cuts the bundle loose, but the slaver puts it back on, keeping it until he reaches the village of his enemies.

On the path he meets a man from the village that knew of his cruelties. The man has a knife. And at first it's not clear what the man will do to his repentant and exhausted enemy. He cuts off the burden once again. This time the former slaver leaves the burden and weeps, and then breaks into joyous laughter. He has been forgiven by God, but he has also now been forgiven by others and can forgive himself.

Often confession and making amends is thought to reveal a misunderstanding of grace, a kind of works or effort to earn God's favor apart from Christ and his cross. But Jesus himself welcomed this kind of confession and restitution. Zacchaeus the tax collector responded to Jesus' message by making amends to all he had defrauded, paying back four times what he had stolen (Luke 19:1-10). Jesus commended him saying, "Today salvation has come to this house." Scholars note that in giving this much away Zacchaeus literally bankrupted himself in repentance. It was a sign that he wasn't just forgiven but he had a whole new life.

Jesus even practiced a kind of confession himself. He submitted to John's baptism, a sign of being repentant for one's sins, as part of his carrying our sin. He didn't have any sin to be baptized for himself but was baptized because of his identification with our sin. Paul says that "God made him who had no sin to be sin for us, so that in him we might become the righteousness of God" (2 Corinthians 5:21). And when he teaches his disciples his way of praying, he includes the request, "Forgive us our trespasses, as we forgive those who have trespassed against us."

Jesus made a practice in his prayer life of identifying with and carrying the sins of others. He takes our pain on himself to heal us of it. And there is a sense that when we enter the pain of those we have hurt and make amends, we join him in carrying his cross. It is not something that earns us God's favor, but it does bring that favor into the living reality of restored relationships.

As part of his practice of making amends, a friend recalled a incident when he was in junior high of stealing a large jar of change from a neighbor. He was using drugs and stole where he could in order to get the high he needed. He was indifferent to the pain he caused others; his only concern was himself. But some memories were coming back as he was doing his daily examination of conscience, not trying to dig up stuff on himself but being open to what God would reveal. This memory was so clear to him that he remembered the dollar amount, $150 in quarters, dimes and nickels.

There is great clarity of why and how making amends will bring restoration and not further harm. It is not a way to impress God or others with the person's goodness but comes from a humble concern for the other person and making things right. When there is this kind of freedom, this practice is full of healing for everyone.

My friend had that kind of freedom as he called on the neighbor some seven years after the incident. He explained why he was at the man's door and matter of factly stated what he had done and what he intended to do about it now. The man was willing to hear the whole story. On a night when my friend was high, he entered the man's house, saw the money and used it for drugs. He wondered if it was savings for the man's wife or children and wanted to replace the $150.

The neighbor was really touched by the courage and care of my friend, but he couldn't remember what the money was for and wanted to forgive my friend. For my friend, restoring the money was important for making amends, so he gave the man the money and told him to do with it what he wanted. The motivation for my friend wasn't feeling better about himself. He wanted to become the kind of person who brought restoration instead of just seeking forgiveness. It was simply an act of obedience.

# Finding Our Rhythm

## *Ninth-Step Work—*
## *Examination and Amends*

Ask two or three trusted family members or friends what attitude or behavior of yours you are blind to that obviously irritates others—an area of life that, if changed for the better, would result in the good of everyone and would make you a better person. Then examine whether you need to make amends with those who shared this with you. What can you own up to and is there any restoration possible? Make amends by apologizing and asking them for ways to make things right in that area. Then act on this information. You'll be better for the effort. Ask these loved ones and friends to help you notice when you exhibit the same attitude or behavior, and work with them to help you change it.

Share the results of your examination and amends with the group the next time you meet. Have someone in the group pray for you and help you discern further growth in making amends.

## *Seeing Widows and Orphans: Psalm 68*

May God arise, may his enemies be scattered;
 may his foes flee before him.
As smoke is blown away by the wind,
 may you blow them away;
as wax melts before the fire,
 may the wicked perish before God.
But may the righteous be glad
 and rejoice before God;
 may they be happy and joyful.

Sing to God, sing praise to his name,
 extol him who rides on the clouds—
his name is the LORD—
 and rejoice before him.
A father to the fatherless, a defender of widows,
 is God in his holy dwelling.
God sets the lonely in families,
 he leads forth the prisoners with singing;
 but the rebellious live in a sun-scorched land.

When you went out before your people, O God,
 when you marched through the wasteland,

the earth shook,
 the heavens poured down rain,
before God, the One of Sinai,
 before God, the God of Israel.
You gave abundant showers, O God;
 you refreshed your weary inheritance.
Your people settled in it,
 and from your bounty, O God, you provided for the poor.
  (vv. 1-10)

When you ascended on high,
  you led captives in your train;
  you received gifts from men,
even from the rebellious—
  that you, O LORD God, might dwell there.

Praise be to the Lord, to God our Savior,
  who daily bears our burdens.

Our God is a God who saves;
  from the Sovereign LORD comes escape from death.
     (vv. 18-20)

THE PSALM PICTURES GOD as a warrior who rides the clouds, but his war is with the conditions of our fallen world, where the powerful and privileged often ignore and even abuse the weak and poor. And the way the psalmist knows this is because of what God has done in rescuing the Israelites themselves from slavery and poverty (v. 10).

This psalm reminds me that God looks out for the overlooked, the vulnerable and the oppressed. The reason is not that one is better in his eyes than the other. The reason is that the oppressor is in the grasp of evil—God's release of the captives is also an invitation to the oppressor to be free as well.

The psalm asks, do we see who God sees, the overlooked who are right nearby in our city or its margins? Are we part of God's delivering grace or part of the oppressive system? How can we join him in setting people free from conditions of poverty and oppression?

This warrior King is a father to the fatherless and a defender of widows. He sets the lonely in families and sets people free from their prisons. He daily bears our burdens and saves people from oppression and death. God expects Israel to join his mission and call the nations to serve the Lord. Although the psalm doesn't present the full kingdom picture of peace, it is a bright light reflecting Christ's peace to come to the whole earth.

The psalm's historical setting is Israel's exodus from Egypt. Moses is called by God to confront Pharaoh, because God has "seen the misery of [his] people" and has "heard them crying out because of their slave drivers" (Exodus 3:7). God sees and hears the poor, the widow and the orphan.

- Take some time this month to go online or to read your city's newspaper and make notes on the burdens of your city's poor and disadvantaged. What ethnic groups suffer on the margins of your city? What needs do they have?

- Prayerfully go through your day, asking God to reveal to you who around you is overlooked or even somewhat invisible to others. How could you pay attention to them? A smile, a greeting, some loving acknowledgment of them or what they do, or just a prayer you silently offer up for their blessing?

- Notice those who you may usually take for granted—a cashier at the store who you could make eye contact with and thank, a neighbor, someone at work, or a stranger on the margins you could show kindness to.

# 10

## Going to Be with the Poor

*Whatever you did for one of the least of these
brothers and sisters of mine, you did for me.*

MATTHEW 25:40 (NIV 2011)

*Only in heaven will we see how much we owe to the poor
for helping us to love God better because of them.*

MOTHER TERESA

Larry is the pastor of a church in a medium-sized city in the Midwest. He was fulfilling the requirement for the doctor of ministry course I taught to make a "pilgrimage to meet Jesus in the least." I found that most of my students had never had contact with the poor, and many had never been to the urban areas where poverty often seems to be concentrated. So I made it a course requirement that they spend a day at a soup kitchen or food pantry or in criminal court—places where the poor and disadvantaged are overrepresented, to observe and be in the presence of those whom Jesus called the "least," people on the margins and in desperate situations.

Many chose to go to their city's criminal court and saw people from all walks of life, although most were from an ethnic minority.

One student reported on the case of a Caucasian man and woman. The man, a well-dressed real estate agent, was in court for violating his ex-girlfriend's restraining order. His lawyer stood beside him ready to help but mostly tried to keep the man from interrupting and frustrating the judge.

The woman, also well-dressed, was visibly upset, frightened and angry at her old lover as he tried to blow the whole thing off as if nothing had happened. He openly showed contempt for her, calling her a "hysterical nutcase" whom he had spent too much on. The judge, after slamming down his gavel and threatening the man with contempt of court, asked some questions of both. Then, showing no particular favor to either, the judge ordered the man to serve some time for his violation. The student observing this couple noted that money and privilege seemed to give the man a false sense of his own power and influence. The man was quite unaware of who was in control in the courtroom.

Another student wrote about an African American man who was to be sentenced for driving while under the influence. He was sincerely sorry and told the judge that he was still mourning the death of his wife and suicide of his son, all in the past year. He had lost his job just before he had gone out drinking. The judge noted that his record was clean except for a drinking and driving charge when he was a young man, and seemed to sympathize with the man. The student said the man was accompanied by a caring neighbor and his wife who the judge allowed to speak on behalf of the man, and after a stiff warning to get some help through Alcoholics Anonymous or some other treatment center, the judge gave the man the most lenient of sentences.

For most of the students, whose pastorates were in suburban churches, the day in court or at a soup kitchen was an eye-opener or at least a reminder of the trouble people could get into. We ended the class with a meditation of Matthew 25's judgment scene about our responsibility to care for the least and the lost. In their reflection pa-

pers many of the students wrote that they started the day with stereo-
types and attitudes they were unaware of until confronted with the
difficult situations people faced. But most of all they reported that
God had reminded them of the humanity of each person in the court,
and by the end of the day they were moved by how sin destroyed and
ruined lives, and how we all need God's grace. They perceived that
the church needs to get out of its ghetto and be involved with those
without Christ, especially those he called "the least of these."

Larry picked a ministry called Emmaus House, which was the only
food shelter in their small Midwestern town. His responsibility was to
assemble bags of food consisting of instant potatoes, a cake mix, cans
of fruit and vegetables and some ramen noodles. He was one of three
volunteers and three paid staff members responsible for the day's
activities.

He noticed that those in need came from all walks of life. There
were the very young, teens, young adults with children, single parents, single pregnant women, middle-aged men and women and a high
number of senior adults. Some appeared healthy but down on their
luck, needing some temporary help. Others were obviously caught up
in a downward cycle of generational poverty and homelessness. Some
were regulars on a first-name basis with the staff. Others were new,
filling out applications for the first time.

They came from all ethnicities, with Caucasians, Latinos and African Americans making up the majority of those requesting food. Some
were well-dressed and others wore torn and dirty clothes. Some were
very thankful and others took the food without a word—perhaps embarrassed or ashamed of their need. Larry took his responsibility seriously and was getting into the swing of food distribution when he was
hit with a bombshell.

Out of the corner of his eye he thought he recognized one of the
recipients. A closer look revealed that it was one of the widows in his
congregation who had several family members in town as well. Vari-

ous thoughts filled his head. *What is she doing here? Why didn't we (her church) know about this need? Why isn't her family helping her?* He was convicted, ashamed and embarrassed all at the same time. As he wrote in his paper, "It was a wakeup call to see that the poor were hidden in my own congregation." He had to go to the margins to find that some on the margins had been right in front of him all along.

Since then Larry has led his church in addressing these needs. His church is now pondering how they can be involved in meeting the needs of the poor in his community.

Albert Nolan uses four stages to describe the typical experiences people have with the poor. First, there is the compassion stage, where interaction with the poor is about feeding, clothing and helping them with resources of money, time and talents. This is done through mission trips, service projects and by developing charitable organizations that do this work.

The second stage represents those who address the causes of poverty and fixing what can be fixed. These people have moved beyond trying to alleviate poverty's impact to go after what gives birth to poverty in the first place. They are concerned with the structural and systemic forces at work that keep people in poverty. They advocate for the poor and try to change their plight by studying justice issues, taking on a cause, fighting for legislative reform, and marching and organizing on behalf of the poor. Those at the third stage are less concerned about activity with or on behalf of the poor, and more concerned with the inward journey, realizing that all the charity and structural work have come from a distance and from the perspective of the poor's deficits rather than their assets. They have come to a more humble assessment of the poor, not looking on them with condescending pity but with dignity.

The fourth stage represents those who see the poor as more like themselves than different. They realize that the poor have the resources of will and determination, and must be involved in discerning problems of poverty and providing possible solutions. They also see the poor with their faults and lose their romantic idealization of poverty.

When we are mentored by the poor, a profound humbling takes place. Befriending the poor—not as a project but as mutual learners—leads to being poor in spirit and cultivating relationships of mutuality. People who identify with the poor desire to become poor—not in a romantic sense of being poor just for the sake of being poor, but to simplify and live less for things and more for people. This was the experience, for example, of Francis of Assisi and Mother Teresa, who are now seen as part of the poor themselves.

Larry's experience involved all of these in some way. And although as a result of Larry's experience, his church is now entering the first quadrant, Larry saw that the poor were no longer "them" but, in a shocking wakeup call of seeing the widow from his church at Emmaus House, he saw them as "us." Larry's experience might lead him to question laws and systems that keep widows in poverty, and he might even begin to see the widow as a mentor in what it means to be "poor in spirit."

## ONE OF US

A popular song in the nineties was titled "One of Us" by Joan Osborne. The song's lyrics wondered what God's experience might be if he was one of us, a stranger who had to take the bus to get home, who struggles like we do. In light of God's incarnation in Jesus, this song is ironic. It reflects our Christ-forgetting but Christ-haunted culture, which still longs for God but has lost the gospel of his son, Jesus. Jesus intentionally never owned anything—no property, no house, no inheritance, no tomb to be buried in. He was born among domestic animals; his bed was a feeding trough.

His first visitors were some of the poorest of the poor, shepherds, and when his parents presented him at the temple, they could only afford the cheapest of sacrifices, two ordinary doves, a concession for those without means. He grew up a refugee, his family fleeing to Egypt and living there awhile as resident aliens. And it appears he was a journeyman carpenter in the poor village of Nazareth, which was an object of scorn.

Jesus' father probably died sometime after Jesus was twelve, and if so, he knew firsthand what it meant for a widow, his mother, to be dependent on others. His observation of the widow who gave everything, mere pennies, to the temple wasn't just a study of poverty, it was his own family's experience. Jesus' whole life was one of being poor. Supporters like Lazarus, Mary and Martha funded his mission, but he didn't use it for himself.

Jesus so identified with the poor that he said when we give a cup of water to a poor person, we do it to him as well. Going to the poor and being with them is being with Jesus. I have found that Jesus is very much with the poor. I used to think I was somehow bringing his presence to them. After getting to know homeless people, I ask them how they make it from day to day. More often than not I find they have a strong faith in God.

On one of my pilgrimages to the poor of our city, I met a man named Trinidad. As he gave my church staff a tour of his part of the inner city, he had a strange greeting for people who were walking by. He would say with a big smile, "Hey, you dropped something!" They would look behind them, check a pocket and then in confusion, look back at Trinidad. Then he would smile even more and say, "You dropped your smile!"

This usually brought a smile to those we met. I asked Trinidad how he had become so positive, and he told me that he had once been quite an angry man. Once, when he was about to murder his brother's killer in a park, a teenage kid in a wheelchair changed his life by hearing him out. The teenager challenged his plan and pointed out how it would change Trinidad for the worse. The teen then told

Trinidad of God's love and asked him, "So, when did you stop smil-ing?" Ever since then, Trinidad had been helping others get their smiles back.

My own wakeup call came as I noticed the many times the psalms say that God meets the needs of widows, orphans, the poor, the needy and the oppressed. I had asked to have a heart like God's and now wanted to see who he saw, who got his attention. I wondered to myself who was oppressed around me. My family and the neighbors in our semi-rural/suburban bubble and most of those I knew at church didn't fit the description.

When I asked God to reveal the poor and needy around me, he gave me new eyes. As I read the paper about gang shootings in a part of our town that I had avoided, I found myself drawn to their names and began to pray for them. They suddenly became the orphans, widows and the needy. This led to an interest in that area of town, which God matched with some opportunities for service there.

Soon I was interested in the systemic problems of that area. I stud-ied the demographics and spent time there. Several years later, after having been on the board of a community development project in the area, I got to know some of the people who lived in this area. My prejudices were exposed and my condescending attitude gave way to a sense of poverty in my own life and richness in theirs. I no longer saw them as objects of my charitable causes or even as the oppressed that needed me as an advocate. I saw them as brothers and sisters in Christ or as human beings made in the image of God. I saw that they had great capacity to help themselves and others. They had resources that I could never give them, but I could stand alongside them in the strug-gle we both had to trust God.

I had my own unintended visit to the margins when as a young seminarian I had to sit for an hour in traffic court. I noticed that most of those in the room were Hispanic. The judge, a Caucasian male, was obviously not happy with his job, and over time, I increasingly noticed his contempt for Hispanics. After the clerk called a person to the bench, the judge would call each one José.

To him they were just a bunch of Josés, not persons. When the clerk called my name and the judge looked up at me, his whole tone and manner changed. "Mr. Meyer, what can we do for you today?" I handily won my case, and then he was back at it, calling out José and dealing "justice" to people he despised.

One of my mentors in this journey, mainly through his writings and speaking, is John Perkins. He was converted to Christ after coming to grips with his own prejudice during the 1960s when he was imprisoned and beat up by police who also murdered his brother. His anger and contempt drove him to Christ and changed his life. He knows that a change of heart is the key, but there also must be changes in social structures and laws.

He gives the example of why charity alone isn't enough, likening it to giving a poor person a fish rather than teaching him or her how to fish. But he takes it further. Even better than teaching a person to fish is helping that person develop the capacity to buy the pond! He also uses an illustration that takes in all of Nolan's four quadrants. Someone by a river sees a nonstop flow of wounded and dying people floating by. Perkins said that the person would undoubtedly get others to help rescue these people, but after a while it should occur to the rescuers that something was happening further up the river and someone should find the source of those being hurt. Perkins likened this person to those who work to alleviate the symptoms of poverty.

But eventually those who go to the source of the problem find out why these people are in the condition they are in and choose to also live in those conditions to improve them. And that requires identifying with them and their plight. For most of us, though, the first step is to take some time to be with the poor and hear God's call to us to do our part in his kingdom work on their behalf.

# Finding Our Rhythm

## *A Day in Criminal Court or a Food Ministry*

As a group decide where you can go to experience life on the margins. Find your city's criminal court and note its schedule so you can spend a day observing the lives played out before the court. Or find a food ministry where you can serve for a day. Listen for how God is speaking to you as you take time to be with the least in this small way. Read Matthew 25 before you go and after you come back. Reflect on what you saw and how it affected you. Share your experience with the group.

## Enjoying God's Good Life: Psalms 111–112

Praise the LORD.
I will extol the LORD with all my heart
    in the council of the upright and in the assembly.

Great are the works of the LORD;
    they are pondered by all who delight in them.
Glorious and majestic are his deeds,
    and his righteousness endures forever.
He has caused his wonders to be remembered;
    the LORD is gracious and compassionate.
He provides food for those who fear him;
    he remembers his covenant forever.
He has shown his people the power of his works,
    giving them the lands of other nations.
The works of his hands are faithful and just;
    all his precepts are trustworthy.
They are steadfast for ever and ever,
    done in faithfulness and uprightness.
He provided redemption for his people;
    he ordained his covenant forever—
    holy and awesome is his name.

The fear of the LORD is the beginning of wisdom;
    all who follow his precepts have good understanding.
    To him belongs eternal praise. (Psalm 111)


Praise the LORD.

Blessed is the man who fears the LORD,
    who finds great delight in his commands.
His children will be mighty in the land;

the generation of the upright will be blessed.
Wealth and riches are in his house,
    and his righteousness endures forever.
Even in darkness light dawns for the upright,
    for the gracious and compassionate and righteous man.
Good will come to him who is generous and lends freely,
    who conducts his affairs with justice.
Surely he will never be shaken;
    a righteous man will be remembered forever.
He will have no fear of bad news;
    his heart is steadfast, trusting in the LORD.
His heart is secure, he will have no fear;
    in the end he will look in triumph on his foes.
He has scattered abroad his gifts to the poor,
    his righteousness endures forever;
    his horn will be lifted high in honor.

The wicked man will see and be vexed,
    he will gnash his teeth and waste away;
    the longings of the wicked will come to nothing. (Psalm 112)

I USED TO THINK THAT BEING HOLY primarily meant growing in morality. The biblical admonition to "be holy because I . . . am holy" (Leviticus 19:2) made me imagine that God had a score card for each of us, keeping track of how our behavior matched up with his commands. I now know that being holy is much more about becoming merciful, and the greatest command is to love one another as God has loved us. Our behavior matters, and so does morality, but not as some of kind of record to look at. It reveals how much of God's love we are allowing in our lives. And the sign of really becoming good is how merciful we are with others. Psalms 111 and 112 teach this truth.

These two psalms are to be read together like we saw with Psalms 130–131 and Psalms 4–5. In Psalm 111 God is described as compassionate, gracious and our provider. Psalm 112 describes the righteous or holy person as also being compassionate and gracious, caring for the poor. Both psalms deal with what it means to "fear the Lord," making clear that the wise person delights in God's commands; that is, he or she is gracious and compassionate with others. And it is from the heart that this person lives and reflects the heart of God.

As we grow into the life God wants for us, it is our heart's desire to love others, not our moral record, that counts. In the end, God wants to see in us compassion for others, the same compassion he has for us (Psalm 111:4-5; 112:4-5).

- What recurring weaknesses and character issues do you struggle with as you seek to follow God?

- What gains have you seen in your struggle in these areas? What is your sense of God's compassion for you in these areas? How have these helped to make you more humble and compassionate toward others?

- What is your sense of God's desires for you in these areas? How much more effective could you be in your capacity to love others in these areas?

- How has God worked in you despite your struggles? How have you been reminded that when you are weak, he is strong?

# 11

# Using a Weakness
# to Cultivate a Strength

*Simon, Simon, Satan has asked to sift you as wheat.*
*But I have prayed for you, Simon, that your faith may not fail.*
*And when you have turned back, strengthen your brothers.*

LUKE 22:31-32

*Growth begins when we begin to accept our own weakness.*

JEAN VANIER

*J*gnatius of Loyola recorded his conversion in a journal that he allowed his followers to publish. He doesn't refer to himself in the first person but uses the third person, calling himself a pilgrim. The pilgrim went here or there, said this or that, did this or that. His refusal to refer to himself was part of his struggle to deflect his ego and pride, hoping, by God's grace, for humility to be miraculously embodied in him.

It is one sign among many of Ignatius's slow change of character, a change that directed his own creative practice of the disciplines, his exercises. As a soldier Ignatius was more concerned with defending God and country than with defeating the pride that separated him from God and others. He had the blessed misfortune of being hit in the leg by a cannonball, which left it with an ugly and repulsive bump. So he could no longer wear his fashionable tight-fitting boots. He couldn't abide going through life looking like that—his appearance was too much a part of his person.

After the bones had been set and healed, he asked his doctor to rebreak the bones, saw off the piece that was sticking out and reset the leg. The doctor warned him that this would require a long process of excruciating lengthening applications, a procedure worse than any pain he had known from the cannonball or the rebreaking of the bones. He was determined to endure the pain and he did. While recuperating in bed, Ignatius read. The only books on hand were a few popular tales of knights, a book about the lives of Christian saints and a copy of the Gospel story of Jesus.

While reading, he noticed that the happiness he found in reading of the glorious adventures of the knights was short-lived and left him feeling empty afterward. But when he read the lives of the saints, even though their lives of humility had no attraction for him at first, he experienced a peace that stayed with him and grew with each reading. The life of Jesus became alive to him, and he imagined being in the stories to experience Christ, just as he had with stories of glorious battles and warriors.

Soon Ignatius decided to convert and make confession to a priest for a new start in life. And that resulted in a change. He became consumed with God's glory in Christ and living for Jesus instead of himself. But that change didn't occur overnight. He recounts in his journal that early in his postconversion life the pilgrim had encountered a Moor who somehow slighted him, and the pilgrim took offense not only for himself but for his country and church! His anger at the Moor grew as he meditated on what happened. And he almost decided to go back to kill him.

But something checked his flaming desire to spill blood once more.

Remembering Christ's life and the saints, he wondered if this was the right thing to do. He was a bit confused by his divided heart. So he prayed and decided to let go of his desire to kill and put it into God's hands. He let go of the reins of his horse and trusted that God would turn the horse around if God wanted Ignatius to kill the Moor. The horse didn't turn, and Ignatius continued his journey. This was one more step in Ignatius's learning to humbly do God's will and be formed in Christ's character.

Ignatius increasingly became aware of his need to sense God's will, realizing that he was under the influence of sin and the evil one more than he knew. His *Spiritual Exercises* were developed as a way for him to discern God's will and to obey Christ as readily as he had obeyed as an officer in the military. He began to humbly live for Christ's honor, not his own.

Ignatius shared these exercises with others and found the exercises significantly helped with their spiritual growth. However, because the church was suspicious of the laity, he was jailed several times. Ignatius learned that Christ's way was one of suffering and humiliation. In his exercise on the way of Christ's passion he explains that anyone following Jesus needs to expect to face the same losses, three in particular—losses of riches, reputation and pride. But these losses are nothing for those who are willing to share in Christ's suffering.

## A PATH OF LOSS

At one Ignatian retreat I attended, I was going through one of the toughest times in my ministry. I was being accused by someone who reported to me that I was not doing my job well. And it didn't look like my supervisors would be on my side. I had learned to trust God through a previous situation like this in which I did not defend myself, and God had vindicated me through a supernatural intervention. This time, though, it looked hopeless. I was facing an ignoble resignation or worse, being fired, which would not look good on my résumé. And if

I couldn't find a new job soon enough, we could lose our home.

The situation was wearing on me and I didn't face it as well as the last time. I got angry and defensive after one incident and was surprised and disappointed in myself. I thought I had done some powerful work on anger and contempt, but the stress was causing more of what was buried down deep to rise to the surface. I had a much harder time trusting God. I really needed a retreat.

I looked forward to the retreat, fully expecting to be refreshed. But the retreat just brought up all the anger and resentment at God for letting things go the way they had. Why hadn't he come through for me as he had in the past? This retreat was becoming a wrestling match between me and God, which wasn't what I expected and wasn't bringing me the comfort I was looking for. God wasn't speaking to me, and I desperately needed to hear his voice, to feel his presence in my trouble.

Eventually, I did. But it wasn't like the comfort I had experienced in the past. This time I had no assurance that everything would turn around. In fact, I felt sure that God had me on the path Ignatius said would come to those who followed Jesus, loss of riches (my job and maybe my home), loss of reputation (being fired) and loss of pride (*I* lose). There was a strange peace that settled over me and ended my struggle at the retreat. God cares more about our character than he does our comfort. He was schooling me, and the question was whether I would be his student.

God was assuring me that he would be with me through it all. And I was thankful for Ignatius, for his imitation of Christ's life and for his *Exercises*. I was thankful for God's work with us in our weaknesses, where he can make us virtuous and strong for others. I eventually did lose my job and was let go. But I had the comfort that God was still with me, and I had an opportunity to learn humility and submission to God's will. Since then I have been able to minister to the many in ministry who find themselves in the same spot.

## JESUS KNOWS

Though sinless, Jesus submitted to all the sufferings we know as human beings in a fallen world. He knew all our emotions, pains and temptations but never let these take him to a place where he chose to do life without his Father. Every test brought him closer to the ultimate obedience of his death, without one fall or failure. I used to feel that his sinlessness lessened his ability to sympathize with me in temptation. But I was helped by C. S. Lewis, who said "only those who try to resist temptation know how strong it is." Jesus' fight with sin was like a champion boxer who goes all twelve rounds with a fierce opponent, whereas my fight with sin is like a boxer who goes down after a few punches in the first round.

This is why he is able to sympathize with us. He knows the full extent of temptation, and on the cross he even submitted to knowing sin's full penalty of guilt, shame and separation from God. It is why we, like Ignatius, can dare to imitate him, knowing that although we will fail, Christ will be tenacious in helping us keep on fighting with sin until, with him, we are victorious.

In Luke 22:31-32, Jesus hints at what he was praying for in his times going off to be alone with the Father. Just after Jesus predicted that one of the disciples would betray him, the disciples try to guess who would do such a thing. Then they launch switch from who would betray Jesus to which of them was greatest and would rule with Jesus.

I can imagine the conversation: "I would never do such a thing; don't you know that Jesus trusted me to be with him when he did some of his most powerful miracles? I am one of his top three." Peter may have been the one bragging the most, for he is singled out by Jesus, who tells him of the test to come upon him. Jesus doesn't call him *Peter*, the Rock, the name Jesus had given this disciple when he had made his great confession of Jesus' messiahship. Jesus calls him by his old name. "Simon, Simon, Satan has asked to sift you as wheat. But I have prayed for you, Simon, that your faith may not fail. And when you have turned back, strengthen your brothers" (Luke 22:31-32).

Jesus did not expect Peter to be perfect but wanted Peter to submit his weakness to God for his ongoing perfecting. Jesus still saw in Peter all the potential he had for powerful ministry. Peter tried to exercise control in the garden of Gethsemane by chopping off one of the guard's ears (John 18:10). But then the sifting began when he saw that Jesus was not going to fight. Later that night Peter denied he knew Jesus.

Later Peter "turns" and preaches and teaches until he is arrested, imprisoned and threatened with death. After he was miraculously set free, he became a rock of strength for the church.

Nevertheless, Peter's weakness wasn't entirely gone. Though Peter had learned from a dream that all foods were now clean for Christ's followers (Acts 10:15), while in Antioch Peter reverted to his weak and mercurial old self. When a controversy erupted in the church at Antioch over whether Gentile believers should have to obey the Jewish ceremonial laws, Paul had to chide Peter for refusing to eat with Gentiles who didn't observe the ceremonial laws, even though Peter himself had stopped following them (Galatians 2:11-14).

Peter's weakness may have followed and dogged him all his life. A tradition in the apocryphal work *The Acts of Peter* says that just before he was martyred in Rome, Peter had another weak moment and tried to flee the city to escape death. As he was going on the road away from Rome, he met Jesus, who was going toward Rome. Peter fell on his knees and asked Jesus, "Quo vadis?" (Where are you going?) Jesus answered him, "To go and be crucified again in Rome." Peter says, "Lord, I will go with you!" Then Jesus ascended to heaven. So Peter turned back to his death, believing that Jesus meant that he would be with Peter as he was martyred.

In 2 Peter we see Peter the Rock again, writing about his own death, which he knows will be soon. He is confident in the first chapter of "[receiving] a rich welcome into the eternal kingdom of our Lord and Savior Jesus Christ" when he puts aside "the tent of this body" (2 Peter 1:11, 13). "Our Lord Jesus Christ has made [this] clear to me," he writes (2 Peter 1:14). Jesus is with us and strengthens us in our weakness, building in us true character as we trust him to make us strong.

Paul also faced times of weakness. He was continually opposed by those he was seeking to win for Christ, especially the Jews. At a time when Paul may have felt like quitting Jesus appeared to him and said, "Do not be afraid; keep on speaking, do not be silent. For I am with you, and no one is going to attack and harm you, because I have many people in this city" (Acts 18:9-10). Jesus' use of Paul weakness caused Paul to glory in his weaknesses (2 Corinthians 12:9-10).

On another occasion Jesus encouraged Paul again to not let his weakness hold him back from ministry.

> [The Lord] said to me, "My grace is sufficient for you, for my power is made perfect in weakness." Therefore I boast all the more gladly about my weaknesses, so that Christ's power may rest on me. That is why, for Christ's sake, I delight in weaknesses, in insults, in hardships, in persecutions, in difficulties. For when I am weak, then I am strong. (2 Corinthians 12:9-10)

I sometimes have the same temptation to quit because of my weaknesses. My active imagination and ability to communicate can result in a lack of good listening, with me always having too much to say too soon. My leadership abilities also have a shadow side—I am too taken with my way, my plans, and I start to become controlling and manipulative. Like Paul, I do better when God has me on an aggressive deliverance program from my faults and character defects. Like Peter, I can be both strong and weak, but so weak sometimes that I doubt my progress and am tempted to give it all up.

It is a tremendous encouragement to know that Jesus' rhythms, both on earth and after his ascension, include praying and working with his disciples in their weakness, building character in them along the way. In his wisdom God has chosen to use us, as Paul said, as cracked clay jars that show off the glory of Christ through flaws and weaknesses (2 Corinthians 4:7).

# Finding Our Rhythm
## *Taking a Virtue Walk*

Peter has some instructions for us in 2 Peter 1:5-8, where he lists areas that need to change in our life; it's a virtue walk. As he learned to trust God, he learned that he could not only begin to walk on water but also walk in obedience to Christ. Although he knew he would do so weakly and defectively until perfected in heaven, God would use him and make him productive, even in his weakness. He says in 2 Peter 1:5-7 to add to our unformed "faith" the following seven qualities or aspects: goodness, knowledge, self-control, perseverance, godliness, brotherly kindness and love.

We can imagine an area of character growth and apply these seven aspects to our faith in God to bring change to us. Take anger for example, and think of the seven aspects. What would a vision of life that is *good* look like if we weren't inappropriately angry? Would we be more patient or gentle? What can we *know* about anger from Scripture—and how it is damaging to us? Why do we have anger? What disciplines can we practice to get *self-control* over it? What challenges will you face in order to *persevere* in your struggle with anger? How can your life reflect more of Christ's lack of anger and move toward *godliness*? What will have to change in your experience of anger so that you are more *kind* in relationships? When you grow in not being angry, how will you *love* those who are?

Review the attitude, behavior or area of your life that your loved ones and group helped you identify (see the exercise in chapter 9). Take a virtue walk in that area by following these steps.

1. Develop a vision of what that attitude, behavior or area of life would look like for you if it were fully under God's rule. Ask your group to help by sharing what they would envision life to be like in this area if it reflected God's best in all of us. (Adding *moral virtue* or a vision of a virtue in practice.)

2. Search the Scriptures to see what they say about that attitude, behavior or area of your life and how we should deal with it. Ask your group to help you with what they might know about what the Scriptures and human experience teach about how to change this area. (Adding *knowledge* of goodness.)

3. What kind of training disciplines can you practice to be able to easily do what you want in this attitude, behavior or area of your life? Ask your group for advice. (Adding *self-control* and training.)

4. Keep up your practice, knowing that your struggle will probably intensify. Things may get worse as you really get after it, but then you should see some growth. (Adding *perseverance* in daily life.)

5. As you persevere, at first you probably will seem to get worse, but that only means you have really begun to deal deeply with this attitude, behavior or area of your life. The first measure of your progress is not your performance but how much more you begin to lean into God for his grace and help. Stay at it; you will eventually see

yourself getting better. (Adding *godliness* or abandonment to God's grace and enabling.)

6. The second measure of your progress in this attitude, behavior or area of your life is that you find yourself growing in your capacity to have a more loving influence on others, not making your growth a performance for God but a way to be more loving, more like him. (Adding *brotherly kindness*.)

7. The final measure of your progress is that you continue in this vision and practice of virtue even when others might resist the changes in you, and you continue to treat them in love. (Adding *agape* or unconditional *love*.)

Have each person in your group share his or her vision (step one) for how he or she would like to change this area of life and what practice or practices (step three) he or she will be using to move into this vision of life.

# Safe Journey Home: Psalm 121

I lift up my eyes to the hills—
    where does my help come from?
My help comes from the Lord,
    the Maker of heaven and earth.

He will not let your foot slip—
    he who watches over you will not slumber;
indeed, he who watches over Israel
    will neither slumber nor sleep.

The Lord watches over you—
    the Lord is your shade at your right hand;
the sun will not harm you by day,
    nor the moon by night.

The Lord will keep you from all harm—
    he will watch over your life;
the Lord will watch over your coming and going
    both now and forevermore.

THIS PSALM REMINDS ME that God is journeying with me as I go through life. And he is available for the journey of each day, through all seasons of life. The Maker of heaven and earth is my personal guardian! He will not fall asleep on the job but will bring me safely home to be with him forever. Death is only a door that he will take me through to be at his side.

This is another of the psalms of ascents used by pilgrims making their way to Jerusalem for the feasts. There is a strong sense of the Lord's care for us, with the word *keep* or *watch* being repeated six times, an unusual thing in the psalms, especially a short psalm like this. God's watch over his own does not refer to his knowledge but of his readiness to help, deliver, protect and provide. His help is as close to us as our right hand. In other words, as soon as we raise it in prayer, he is there to keep us from any harm.

The psalm also uses a poetic device of coupling opposites, such as day and night, sun and moon, waking and sleeping, coming and going. This is not mere parallelism but reveals the scope of God's watchfulness. He keeps us from morning to night and every moment in between.

The word *life* is comprehensive and points to everything in every day of our lives, from our birth to our death and beyond. The psalm tells us that God has his eye on us and a hand ready to help. He is so careful in that watching that we can rest safely all the days of our life, no matter what happens.

- Have you ever wrestled with the psalmist's question, "Where does my help come from" (v. 1)? Describe a situation when you wondered if God was doing his job and you felt alone, unprotected and unsafe.

- How has God kept you—watched over you and met you during these rough days in your journey?

- Regarding your future, in what areas do feel alone, unprotected or unsafe? What fears of death stir in you? Put these fears into God's hands by praying this psalm over them.

# 12

# MAKING OUR LIFE
# A PILGRIMAGE TO HEAVEN

*Jesus knew that the hour had come for him*
*to leave this world and go to the Father.*

JOHN 13:1

*Jesus makes it clear that for his followers there is*
*no experience or taste of death. When you die it is like passing from*
*one room to another. You might not know you are dead until you*
*see loved ones who you shouldn't be seeing welcoming you.*

DALLAS WILLARD

We don't get to be near people who are dying anymore. Most of them die at hospitals or homes for the elderly, and if we are there, those who die are often so medicated that they slip away in a comatose state. It wasn't always this way. Christians used to expectantly wait with their loved ones who were about to make their earthly exodus to be in the immediate presence of Jesus. It was a sacred space and time in which angels showed up and those about to pass on reported seeing things unseen by those on this side of eternity.

Christians were encouraged to think often of their death, preparing for it by living each day as if it was the last, ready to be with the Lord. Going to bed at night was a time to entrust yourself to God, not just for the next day but as a preparation for your last day. Jeremy Taylor's meditation *Holy Living and Holy Dying* is an example of how life and death were seen as places to engage God and his will for us.

My great-grandmother Louise was one of those who died before there was hospice. She had been bedridden for most of her life and had returned to her faith as a young woman. As she was dying, she suddenly looked up and addressed unseen presences, saying, "Mother! Father! I can see you!" And then with utter delight she said, "Jesus." Then she was gone.

My father often used the story of a parishioner named Ruth as an illustration of the reality of heaven and the hope we have that this life is not all there is. As pastor of a congregation with a large number of elderly, he visited the "shut-ins," those who were unable to come to church. One of those he had regularly visited, Ruth, had died. In preparation for her funeral, he was given her Bible to look for passages she had marked.

In the back cover he found a long list of names that looked like a prayer list with many different requests for each name. There was one word written next to a few of the names after which there were no more requests. The word written next to the names was simply *home*. Ruth had faithfully prayed for her friends and noted when they had gone home to be with Jesus. My father shared this during the funeral message, noting that Ruth was not going to a place where she would be alone but that she would be home with many who had gone on before her to be with her Lord.

My father developed many other wonderful relationships with the elderly in that church. One shut-in, Oscar, had to go to the hospital, where his family thought he would spend his last few weeks of life. They called my father one night when it looked like the end was near, and he arrived ready to pray with them and Oscar, who was ready to meet his Savior.

But when Dad came in the room, Oscar lit up and suddenly found new life. They talked for a while, reminiscing and telling old stories that had been told many times before. Then my father prayed with the family and Oscar for God's peace. Dad went home and presumed that he would soon get a call to arrange this old parishioner's funeral. But no call came. Days passed and Dad inquired about Oscar's condition. Remarkably he had made a recovery—not enough to go home, but he was certainly not knocking on heaven's door anymore.

But a few weeks later, the call came again for Dad to visit Oscar and the family. He was showing the signs of going home that he had before. Once again, Dad spent an evening with Oscar and the family, and once again Oscar's condition went from near death to renewed energy and life. Everyone was surprised at this second recovery. Dad went home expecting that it would be short-lived and the inevitable phone call would soon come.

But Oscar hung on! Some weeks went by and the same pattern repeated: decline, Dad's visit and Oscar's revival. Finally, the family called my father and said, they didn't know if they should call him the next time Oscar looked like he was on his way home. But the next time Oscar didn't revive and he finally went home to be with his Lord.

Oscar and Ruth's stories are reminders that when we die we will not be on our own, alone, having left everyone behind. Like Oscar we might not want to leave our loved ones, or we may be like Ruth, praying herself, her loved ones and her friends safely home. We actually go from one group of friends and loved ones to another, and as my great-grandmother Louise found, there may be a time when we are briefly in touch with those on both sides.

## DEATH AND LIFE

When death is understood from this Christian and biblical perspective, we begin to understand Paul's dilemma: should we prefer to live and be a blessing and of service to those on earth, or should we wish to die and gain the blessing of being directly with Jesus and those who have gone on before us (Philippians 1:21-25)? But for many of us, death is not that kind of doorway. We know that when we die we will be with Jesus, but the reality of that place is largely unknown to us. And the actual event of death is something fearful and full of mystery.

I remember first hearing Dallas Willard describe what it will be like when we die. He asked us, "Do you think you will cease to exist, or slip off to some kind of unconscious sleep until the resurrection?" He then exclaimed, "Why, you may not even know you are dead until you start seeing people you know you shouldn't be seeing or when you meet an angel." Dallas went on to explain that when Jesus said to the Pharisees that anyone who believed in him would never see or taste death (John 8), Jesus meant being separated from God, others and life itself will not be our experience.

Death is now only a door we pass through, like going from one room filled with a bunch of people to another room with another group of people. Jesus presented this same picture of death. Lazarus was deathly ill and his sisters, Mary and Martha, sent messengers to fetch Jesus before it was too late. But Jesus stayed where he was for another two days. When he finally left for Lazarus's home, he was met by the confused and distraught sisters, who are wondering why Jesus didn't come when they called, and who are maybe even a little bit angry and bitter at his delay. Their confusion is understandable—the distance between them and where Jesus was, was a only a few miles.

Jesus explained that his delay was to display God's glory. In other words, his delay would highlight how little power death really has. When Jesus wept at the graveside of his friend Lazarus, it wasn't due to his sorrow for Lazarus; he knew he would be bringing Lazarus back to life. Jesus wept hard because he was angry at the grip death had on those he loved. He was distraught over our fear of death and our ignorance about what it means to be alive to God.

Jesus repeated the same message he had given to the Pharisees about those who have faith in God—they would not taste or see death. To Martha and Mary he said that even though we appear to die, we don't; we live on. Martha responds by saying, "I know he will rise again in the resurrection at the last day" (John 11:24). But Jesus wasn't talking about the future resurrection of the dead, he was talking about Lazarus being alive even as they talked, kept so by God's mighty hand.

Jesus' emotional response to our fear of death is one of the strongest shown in the Gospels. His anger at Lazarus's tomb is rivaled only by his anger when cleansing the temple. He had come to conquer death, the final enemy. One half of Mark's sixteen chapters is about Jesus facing his death and telling his disciples to prepare for it. But this was not a time of morose brooding. Jesus intensely focused on his mission, to live in such a way that death had no control over him and to die in such a way that we too can be fearless about death and fully alive all our days.

Along with the church fathers Origen, Athanasius and Basil of Caesarea, Dallas Willard holds an unusual interpretation of Jesus' prayer to "let this cup pass from me" in the garden of Gethsemane (Matthew 26:39 KJV). They believe the cup referred to being hijacked and ambushed before he was lifted up on the cross. So Jesus was not praying for the cross to be taken away but to be protected until he was nailed onto it and lifted up in a kind of death that would show God's love and forgiveness in its fullest measure. The result of his death would be the death of our fear of death, because God had faced it for us in his Son. Now it is just a door, a passage from one life to another.

John Ortberg shared the following story when giving the funeral meditation for a friend. He was explaining how death was no longer something we have to fear, even though we still do.

When our two daughters were real little we took them one time to a hotel that has a swimming pool. We warned them to not run around the pool; you could drown and that would be really bad. They were taking turns jumping to me, and they were like three and five years old, and Laura was jumping, and Mallory who was three years old, was wiggling around and she fell into the pool . . . all the way in.

I reached down real fast to pull her out, but by the time I reached her, she was already weeping and she said, "Daddy, I drowned, I drowned, I drowned." I said, "No, Mallory, you did not drown. That was not drowning. I was watching you the whole time. You were never in danger. So let's not tell your Mommy about this." Because I knew what she did not know, that her father was watching her and his arms were plenty strong enough to lift her out of the water—just a moment going into the water; she was never in danger.

Jesus taught his disciples the same thing—we are never in danger because we cannot fall any farther than the Father's arms can reach to catch us. He came to deliver us from the fear of death which is behind every fear of loss and the crippling of a life's potential to live in God's life, peace and love. When we begin to trust in this truth our lives become incredibly exciting journeys that show others the way home to life in the kingdom as well as how to live a glorious life at home with God in this life.

I have made a habit and spiritual practice out of this biblical instruction: "Remember your leaders, who spoke the word of God to you. Consider the outcome of their way of life and imitate their faith. Jesus Christ is the same, yesterday and today and forever" (Hebrews 13:7-8). I study the lives of "saints," women and men of God whose faith in God and Jesus and whose life in the Spirit are examples of what this short span of time on earth can be—a spiritual adventure with God. While we are on earth, which is passing away for a new heaven and earth, we can trust in Jesus to be the same for us today and tomorrow as he was for them yesterday. As Paul asked of the Corinthians, all we have to do is follow the saints' example, as they follow Jesus (1 Corinthians 11:1).

## BOUNDARY WATERS

On a trip one summer to the chain of lakes in the Boundary Waters of northern Minnesota, I found a metaphor for what Paul and the writer of Hebrews are suggesting. These saints become for us "living Bibles." They show us how to live and die in hope of our home in heaven.

One of my companions in the Boundary Waters had a map showing the lakes and portage trails. I often found the next portage trailhead before he did by simply watching where others were heading. On one lake he was sure those ahead of us were wrong. Stubbornly, he paddled with his exhausted wife to the place where he thought the trail was. Refusing to treat my wife the same, I waited for him to realize the others were correct and circle back to where we were. That experience has become an illustration of why I don't trust my own skill and experience alone to interpret the Bible. Instead, I look to the lives of those who have gone on before me.

I have read about many of the saints and prayed that I might be able to in some small way follow their examples as they followed Jesus. One particular Puritan saint, Anne Bradstreet, wrote a letter to her children in which she recounted the hellish trial of her sickness and pain. But she also explained how it was a place where God met her with his life and grace.

She admonished her children to draw near to God all their days, no matter what their life's journey brought them, trusting in God's love and following his will. She said that if she were in heaven but God were not there, it would be a hell to her. And if she were to be in hell and found God there, it would be heaven to her. Her intent in writing was to have her children imitate her practice of God's presence and know the same peace, no matter what their lives encountered.

# FINDING OUR RHYTHM
## *Pilgrimage with a Saint*

Take some time in your group for each person to name saints or heroes of the faith that have been examples of growth in love and journeying with God. Make a list of those mentioned. These saints show us how to live and die gloriously. Share why your saint affected you. From this list (or from other saints you know of) have each member of the group pick one person to study, reflect on and imitate. (Alternately, the whole group can study and report on the same saint.) Then, before your meeting, spend time answering the following questions for sharing with your group.

1. In what ways did the saint or hero change through his or her journey with God?

2. What difficulties and trials did the saint suffer through?

3. How did God use this person in the lives of others?

4. What are you drawn to imitate in his or her life?

# CONCLUSION

*Staying in a Place Where You Can Be Found*

*J*ust like Father Harry in the opening of this book, we can and will get lost. Periods of dryness and life's interruptions can knock us off our discipline rhythms.

It is always easier not to get lost when you aren't on your own. When we practice the disciplines together and are formed in the context of our community and mission to others, our experiences of God are some of the most powerful and productive we can experience. But we still can get lost, even when our experience of God and each other is at its most glorious. The disciples had an experience like this with Jesus.

Jesus was in the midst of a group discipline of prayer and solitude when he and three of his disciples, Peter, James and John, experienced a powerful manifestation of God. Sometimes in the regular habit of disciplines the earthly curtain that dims our sight is drawn back to reveal the glory of heaven. On the mount of transfiguration the disciples witnessed the Hebrew Scriptures come alive in the persons of Moses and Elijah, who talked with Jesus about his exodus from earth (Matthew 17:1-11). Their appearance was God's gift of special community to form him for his mission in the days to come.

The three disciples began to plan on enshrining this profound experience by building three huts or shelters so they could all stay on the mountain and bask in this glory. They lost sight of God in the midst of this experience of his glory and wanted to maintain what they were experiencing. They were focusing on the practice of the disciplines rather than on God.

A cloud suddenly enshrouded them and ended their plans. God then said, "This is my Son, whom I love; with him I am well pleased. Listen to him!" (v. 5). God found them in the midst of their confusion and misguided attempts to stay on the mountain of their prayer discipline. Then Jesus led them back to the rest of the Twelve and the next phase of his mission. God the Father had called them back to their focus on Jesus and back to their spiritual rhythms with him—not their experiences of him.

Like the disciples, your spiritual rhythms will allow you to always be found by God and others—whether you are facing dryness, are surprised by a moment of glory or are just living in the routine of every day.

I pray that your spiritual rhythms bring you into fresher and deeper experiences of community and mission. May you and your community be caught up in the dance of the Trinity. And may the heavens open up to your community to see God's great glory in your midst.

Let's keep listening to Jesus together.

# A Guide for Groups

## MEETING SCHEDULES

The book and exercises can be used one of four ways:

- *One quarter (three months) of weekly meetings.* The group meets weekly for twelve weeks to discuss the psalm, chapter and Finding Our Rhythm exercise from the week before. Alternately, the exercise, especially the three day-long exercises, can be done at a meeting scheduled after the reflection and chapter have been discussed.

- *One half year (six months) of weekly meetings.* The group meets weekly for twenty-four weeks and alternates between (1) meeting to discuss the psalm and the chapter, and (2) meeting to discuss their experience with the Finding Our Rhythm exercise for that chapter.

- *One year, meeting twice a month.* The group meets twice a month, first to discuss the psalm reflection and the chapter, and a second time to do or discuss the Finding Our Rhythm exercise.

- *At your group's pace.* The group reads the material and does the exercises at whatever pace fits the group.

## SPECIAL PREPARATION AND PLANNING

To complete three of the chapters (one, five and seven) you will need a day, from morning to late afternoon, on retreat. This will require prior planning by the whole group.

## SAMPLE MEETING OUTLINE

1. *Opening prayer.* Someone in the group recognizes and invites the presence and work of the Trinity—Father, Son and Holy Spirit—to the meeting.

2. *Check in.* In the first meeting, if the group members are new to each other, start with an activity where each group member can briefly share something about themselves, such as their work or favorite leisure activity. If everyone knows each other, find out how the others are feeling as they come to the meeting. "I am coming to the meeting _____ [your condition such as tired, excited, sad, etc.] because_____ [give the reason or circumstance for why you are coming as you are to the meeting]."

3. *Psalm reading/sharing.* Have someone read the psalm for this chapter. Then have the group members share and discuss their answers to the reflective questions.

4. *Chapter discussion.* Share your answers to the following discussion questions.

   • What was the main point or points of the chapter?

   • How does Jesus' life exemplify this chapter?

   • What in the chapter most affected you? Is there something new you learned? An experience you are interested in exploring? A question that was raised for you?

5. *Prepare for the exercise.* How will your group accomplish the exercise? If another meeting is needed, schedule that. If a film needs to be ordered (chapters three and six) or a visit to a court or food pantry arranged (chapter ten), work out those details. Note that information on getting the films and other resources are in the notes.

6. *Closing prayer.* Have a few of the group members express thanks to

God for the meeting experience.

May the words of this book and the exercises we share bring renewal and a refuge to your deepest heart. And may you bless others by sharing that retreat center with them as you let them into your heart or as they knock on the door of your life and ask to join in your happiness in God. You can become a place where they can find God.

# Acknowledgments

$\mathcal{T}$his book would not have happened without the loving support and encouragement of my family and the influence and gifts of others.

My wife, Cheri, and adult children, Kyle, Cara and Mike, illustrate what it means to "write on another's heart" and keep a corporate journal in relational space. It is a rare and precious privilege to have a spouse and children who are not only my best friends but also soul friends who share a common spiritual hunger and pursuit of kingdom life in Christ.

Much of the basis for this book comes from the retreat course I teach in Denver Seminary's Doctor of Ministry program under the direction of Dr. David Osborn and his assistant, Janet Campbell. I am again grateful to them and to the many students in those courses who have shared their stories with me in reflection papers and conversations. Being with them at St. Malo's Retreat Center on the east side of the Colorado Rockies at 9,000 feet is heavenly.

I am grateful to retreat leaders who I have imitated and borrowed from, such as Dallas Willard, Keith Matthews and Jan Johnson (Fuller retreat course at the Passionist Retreat, Sierra Madre, California); Father Jim Deegan and the late Father Basil Pennington (Buffalo Kings House, Buffalo, Minnesota); and various staff who have led me, my family and friends in the Ignatian *Exercises* (Demontreville Jesuit Retreat House in Lake Hugo, Minnesota).

Many of the stories and ideas related to the poor and pilgrimages to the inner city are borrowed from pilgrimages led by Tom Allen, who was executive director of CityHouse in St. Paul, and his coworker Tamie Koehler. I am grateful for Tom and Tamie's influence on my life and ministry, and for bringing me to an understanding of how God is with the poor. Thank you also to Albert Nolan for his four stages, and thanks to Janet Hagberg for her adaptation of them, incorporating Nolan's work with her stages of faith.

I want to thank my first Hebrew studies professor at Wheaton College, Dr. Hassell Bullock, who helped me form a love for the Psalms and the Hebrew language. I also want to thank Gary Moon for his help in encouraging and developing my writing, and for inviting me to be published as a rookie writer. Finally, I cannot adequately express my thanks to my editor, Cindy Bunch, and the team at InterVarsity Press. I am so thankful for Cindy's expertise in organizing and editing books, and for her constant encouragement all the way through the writing process. IVP, you have been so very good to me.

# Notes

### Chapter 1: Getting Alone to Be with the Father

*p. 26*      *I Never Sang for My Father: I Never Sang for My Father,* dir. Gilbert Cates (Burbank, Calif.: Columbia Pictures Corporation, 1970). This film is not available from Netflix or Amazon.com. The original play by Robert Anderson is available on Amazon.com in paperback. To watch a good sample clip go to www.youtube.com/warch?v=6jHeHtnOLe4.

### Chapter 2: Creating a Retreat Center of the Heart

*p. 41*      "Late have I loved Thee": *The Oxford Book of Prayer,* ed. George Appleton (Oxford: Oxford University Press, 1985), p. 65.

*p. 49*      *Storm on the Sea:* Brother Claude Lane, *Storm on the Sea.* This icon is available for purchase at 1-800-889-0105 or www.printeryhouse .org. Used by permission.

*p. 52*      "The Journey" and "Be Still and Know": Steven Curtis Chapman, *Speechless* (Sparrow, 1999).

### Chapter 3: Encountering the Ancient Desert and Postmodern Wild

*p. 56*      "If you want to, you can become all flame": *Becoming Fire: Through the Year with the Desert Fathers and Mothers,* ed. Tim Vivian (Collegeville, Minn.: Liturgical Press, 2008), p. 8.

*p. 60*      *Into the Wild: Into the Wild,* dir. Sean Penn (Los Angeles: Paramount Vantage, 2007), is based on Jon Krakauer, *Into the Wild* (New York: Anchor, 1977). The DVD is available at Netflix and Amazon.com.

### Chapter 4: Going Off-Line

*p. 77*      "Into your hands, O Lord, I commend": Phyllis Tickle, *The Divine Hours: Prayers for Summertime* (New York: Doubleday, 2000), p. 177.

**Chapter 5: Wasting Time Just Being**

*p. 83*        Edwards studied the "flying spiders": Jonathan Edwards, *The Sermons of Jonathan Edwards*, ed. Wilson N. Kimnach, Kenneth P. Minkema and Douglas A. Sweeney (New Haven, Conn.: Yale University Press, 1999), pp. xxiv, 121-40, 242-72.

**Chapter 6: Entering into Quiet**

p. 102        Watching *Into Great Silence: Into Great Silence,* dir. Philip Gröning (Cincinnati: Arte Films, 2005).

**Chapter 7: Writing on Each Other's Hearts**

*p. 113*       Surprisingly, science may back: See the Institute of HeartMath, www.heartmath.org/research/science-of-the-heart/introduction.html.

p. 115        St. Francis and Clare: Susan Saint Sing, *Francis and the San Damiano Cross: Meditations on Spiritual Transformation* (Cincinnati: St. Anthony Messenger Press, 2006).

**Chapter 8: Using Earthly Attachments for a Fix on Eternity**

*p. 128*       "prone to wander Lord, I feel it": Robert Robinson, "Come Thou Fount of Every Blessing" (1758).

**Chapter 10: Going to Be with the Poor**

*p. 152*       Albert Nolan's four quadrants: Albert Nolan, "Spiritual Growth and the Option for the Poor," June 29, 1984, www.maryknollvocations.com/nolan.pdf.

**Chapter 11: Using a Weakness to Cultivate a Strength**

*p. 161*       "only those who try to resist temptation": C. S. Lewis, *Mere Christianity* (London: Fontana Books, 1952), p. 122.

**Chapter 12: Making Our Life a Pilgrimage to Heaven**

*p. 174*       "When our two daughters were real little": Memorial address by John Ortberg at Wheaton College on the death of Dr. Gerald Hawthorne, which is no longer available online.

*p. 175*       I sudy the lives of "saints": See David Aikman, *Great Souls* (Nashville: Thomas Nelson, 1998); Susan Bergman, *Martyrs* (Maryknoll, N.Y.: Orbis, 1998); and by Philip Yancey, *Soul Survivor* (Colorado Springs: Waterbrook, 2003).

# About the Author

*Take Your Next Step into Spiritual Rhythms*

Keith invites you to visit and contact him at his website:
**www.keithmeyer.org**

Learn about the various ways he can resource your life and ministry through speaking, teaching, training seminars, personal coaching and organizational consulting (online, Skype or onsite visits).

He also leads retreats for pastors and their spouses, church staff teams, marketplace leaders and students, and helps in the planning and creation of your own yearly cycles of corporate and individual retreat rhythms.

Create your own life-changing "rule of life" with Keith's coaching and by becoming a practicing member of The Order of the Renovated Heart. This is a cyber-blogging community of apprentices to Jesus sharing their experiences by intentionally envisioning and training to become individual and corporate examples for others—a catching force for God's kingdom.

You can also support the work of training pastors and leaders through contributing to the BTC Foundation.

 **Becoming the Change Ministries** (Nonprofit)
The BTC Foundation
Keith Meyer Consulting, LLC

*"Be the Change That the World Is Waiting to See"*

## formatio
TRADITION. EXPERIENCE.
TRANSFORMATION.

Formatio books from InterVarsity Press follow the rich tradition of the church in the journey of spiritual formation. These books are not merely about being informed, but about being transformed by Christ and conformed to his image. Formatio stands in InterVarsity Press's evangelical publishing tradition by integrating God's Word with spiritual practice and by prompting readers to move from inward change to outward witness. InterVarsity Press uses the chambered nautilus for Formatio, a symbol of spiritual formation because of its continual spiral journey outward as it moves from its center. We believe that each of us is made with a deep desire to be in God's presence. Formatio books help us to fulfill our deepest desires and to become our true selves in light of God's grace.